‖‖‖‖‖‖‖‖‖‖‖‖‖‖‖‖‖‖‖‖‖‖‖‖

☞ **W9-CEK-425**

i

Dedication

This book is dedicated to my wife and our newly born son, and the society that he will inherit.

Life Management Skills Publishing Co. A division of Life Management Skills, Inc.

11340 West Olympic Blvd., Suite 145, West Los Angeles, CA 90064

Copyright © 1994 by Marc F. Kern, Ph.D.

All rights reserved, including the right to reproduce this book,
or portions thereof, in any form whatsoever.

For information address Life Management Skills Publishing Co.
A division of Life Management Skills, Inc.
11340 W. Olympic Blvd., Suite 145, West Los Angeles, CA 90064

Kern, Marc F.

Take Control Now, (Developing Healthy Habits)

Marc F. Kern with Lance Lenon

Library of Congress #94-072846

Life Management Skills Publishing Co. is a registered trademark of
Life Management Skills, Inc.

Printed in the U.S.A.

Note: The author and publishers disclaim any liability arising directly from the use of this book.

Take Control Now!

The Keys for Developing Healthy Habits

TABLE OF CONTENTS

BEGINNING THOUGHTS

The following are passages from Oscar Wilde's famous novel, "A Picture of Dorian Gray." Perhaps they sound enticing, but each is a trap.

"Be always searching for new sensations. Be afraid of nothing. . . A new Hedonism -- that is what our century wants."

"We are punished by our refusals. Every impulse that we strangle broods in the mind and poisons us. The body sins once, and has done with its sin, for action is a mode of purification. Nothing remains but the recollection of a pleasure, or the luxury of a regret."

"The only way to get rid of temptation is to yield to it. Resist it, and your soul grows sick with longing for the things it has forbidden to itself, with desire. . . It has been said that great events of the world take place in the brain. It is in the brain, and the brain only, that the great sins of the world take place. . ."

These sentiments are just as applicable to society today as they were in 1891 when this book was written. The thoughts expressed here are totally wrong, and are the guidelines that seduce us into practicing unhealthy habits. Habits which rob us of the quality and freedom of life. Habits which enslave us. Just like the enchanted painting of himself that Dorian Gray kept hidden away robbed him of all the quality of his life. It was a magical picture that allowed Dorian to stay young and beautiful while he watched the painting itself take on all the burdens of age, sins, and a host of unhealthy behaviors. To him, it was like watching his own soul suffer the torments of the damned.

In our wish to believe that we are taking control, we unwittingly turn down a pathway which leads us into a subservience to our unhealthy behaviors and habits. Although we do not have a picture by which we can watch ourselves change and deteriorate, as Dorian Gray did, we instinctively know that we have become locked in the chains of unhealthy behaviors that are severely reducing the quality of our lives, if not destroying us.

This book was written to act as the key to unlock the bonds that your unhealthy habits have around you. In a self-help manner, you can truly take control of your life in a very realistic and do-able manner, and master these unwanted habits.

It is truly my wish that you will use the pages of this book as the keys for developing healthy life-skills and for adding direction and purpose into your life.

Marc Frederick Kern, Ph.D.

TAKE CONTROL NOW!

PREFACE

There is a thief within each of us -- robbing us of our life. This thief steals our happiness, productivity, health, and self-esteem. As importantly, it steals days, weeks, months, and even years off our lives. Above all that, it undermines life's quality and enjoyment. Amazingly enough, it does this so quietly that we don't even notice, until suddenly it becomes too late. The thief is as much as part of us as our thoughts and our instincts. The thief is our unhealthy lifestyle habits.

"The chains of habit are too weak to be felt until they are too strong to be broken." This quote by Samuel Johnson was first made in the 1700's, but it has greater impact in today's complex, high stress society. Health is not a goal, it is a means to doing what is purposeful and meaningful in life. It is time to engage yourself instead of indulging yourself, it is time to take control! Unhealthy habits can kill us as we go about our daily lives without our even noticing, they simply become the "norm." Unhealthy habits such as smoking, poor stress management skills, over drinking, poor work habits, procrastination, poor study habits, hypochondria, poor self-esteem, poor eating habits, chronic absenteeism, weight control, continuous self doubting, addictive depression, misuse of drugs, compulsive shopping, pornography addiction, not taking prescribed medication properly or on time, and free floating fear are only a few of the overt symptoms of unhealthy lifestyle management techniques. There are also thousands of less obvious habits that we engage in every day. Unhealthy habits affect you or someone you love in the most negative ways. They rob you of the emotional quality of life, cheat you out of many of life's monetary rewards, and most importantly steal your precious time. The worse thing to happen in life is to miss life. Now is the time for clear thinking, not shadow thinking. Take Control, NOW!

The author of this book, Marc Frederick Kern, Ph.D. understands all too well how it feels to be victimized by this thief. He too was enticed into a life dominated by unhealthy habits. Having started his professional career as an Architect he entered the field of Psychology after he mastered his own unhealthy lifestyle habits so that he could focus his energies on helping himself while helping others. Dr. Kern intends this book to be a lifetime training manual for self-management. His views and opinions are founded on the most modern cutting edge of technology and are arranged in such a way to allow the reader to come to know himself/herself and gain important life management skills along the way. He does not want to see bad habits eroding your quality of life.

Dr. Kern is an international speaker and lecturer, he has authored articles in the prestigious 'International Journal of the Addictions,' he is the National Director of Addiction Alternatives, the Founding Director of the Los Angelels Stress and Lifestyle Management Skills Center, and is the Southern California Advisor for the nationally respected Rational Recovery self-help network. He is an active member of many professional associations including the American Psychological Association, and the Society of Psychologists in Addictive Behaviors. Dr. Kern has been a featured guest on a wide variety of radio and television programs, and he has been a consultant to Cable News Network (CNN) regarding psychological matters. He has written this book in order to aid the most important person in your life to bring you out of the repression of your unhealthy habits and back into the world of self-control and healthy lifestyle management. Of course, that person is you, yourself. You are a vessel of valuable cargo, it is unhealthy to keep destructive secret thoughts locked deep in your subconscious, spoiling the valuable contribution to life that you have to offer. Only you know the secret keys that it takes to unlock the chains in which the thief has shackled you.

As you turn the pages of this book, you will climb up the ladder of success and self-esteem once again. There is an old saying that is so true in this case: "IF YOU DO THE SAME OLD THING IN THE SAME OLD WAY, YOU WILL GET THE SAME OLD TIRED RESULTS." This book is not the same old remedy, the same old trodden pathway. This is new and important for you. Read it, follow it, and walk boldly into the light of a new day of emotional freedom.

A PERSONAL STORY

THE BOY'S NEW FRIENDS

He felt that his body was alive, but his soul was dead. There was nothing there. To him, his life was like the stark leafless branches of a dead tree in winter looking like a tormented hand desperately reaching up to a cold gray sky offering no help and no comfort. He was totally alone and he felt it. The loneliness of his life built upon itself creating a vast void of nothingness between him and everyone else. The irony was that he was privileged. He came from a family who had good social position and wealth, but that offered no comfort. In fact, it made it worse. He felt like nothing, while his family, his mother in particular, had personality and zest. She was so outgoing that part of her life's blood was giving lavish parties. In fact, she had become renowned for her parties. He remembered those "party days." As he walked up the darkening evening streets coming home from school he could see the house ablaze with light and he knew that the preparation for the festivities had begun again. Then an infinite sea of sorrow would drown his thoughts. His brain would become numb as he thought about how he would cope with all the guests. He was supposed to be the "apple of his mother's eye," he was supposed to be happy and normal, but how could she see into his secret world, how could anyone know that he was truly alone -- adrift in an ocean of uncertainty with no safe port for shelter. He felt damned to a life of endless hopelessness and he was always alone.

School should have been a refuge with friends and activities. He should have been like any normal boy. In fact he should have had the advantage of coming from a good family, having good looks, and proper breeding. However, in actuality, school was worse. He just didn't seem to have the knack of making friends. He lacked the tools to make lasting social connections with his peers. God knows that he tried, he sent out every signal that he could. He tried to blend in and become a "regular guy" but it just wasn't in the cards for him. His interests simply didn't match those of the others and his basic skills seemed to be lacking as well. He managed to get through his school work, but when it came to participating in sports he just seemed to be naturally un-coordinated. Physical Education class in school is the mortar that bonds young men together. It acts as the first common social ground where they can let down their defenses and make some honest friends. He wasn't good in sports so he became the outcast. It always seems that there has to be one black sheep in the group and unfortunately he realized that it was him. He was the heaviest, the slowest, and the weakest. He was always the last to be chosen to be on teams, so he got picked on, not only by the others, but by the coach as well. He wasn't good, so the coach didn't like him. This was just the crowning blow. Adrift, going nowhere, he became depressed and turned to food for comfort. This offered only temporary relief and had the terrible side effect of making him more overweight and an even greater target for the others to ridicule and push farther away. He knew that when he ate, he felt better. But he only felt better during the time when he was actually eating the food. After he ate, he would always think about what he had done and hate himself even more for taking the easy way out and making himself fatter in the process. He soon came to realize that even his thoughts were becoming his enemies. Nothing he thought about would make him feel better. He knew that he couldn't change his thoughts so he had to find a way to change his feelings. If he couldn't think his way out, then he would feel his way out.

Looking for the good feelings that he received when he ate, he looked for other things, other relationships that would give him this same feeling. It was at this point that the big lie began, and the unhealthy habits took over his entire lifestyle. He started living the 'short-cut life.'

It wasn't until his freshman year in college that he was introduced to "pot." He had finally connected with a group that was involved in the drug culture that was just on the rise at that time. He liked them because they were friendly to him, he was so naive that he didn't know that their lifestyle truly centered around drugs.

Although he was not a religious person, pot became a spiritual experience for him. In fact, it became the foundation that held up the flimsy framework of his life. It became his meaning to life, and his vehicle to adulthood. He had tried it at first just to please his new friends. How was he to have known that it would change his whole life. The pleasures of pot offered him a soft cushion that insulated him from what he saw as the horror of real life. Suddenly he had friends with common interests, and suddenly much of life's pain seemed to be blurred and not connected to him. He lied to himself with the thought that this was good.

In actuality, he was barely making the grades to stay in school. His major was Architecture, a field that he had chosen because it held the promise of good pay and social position -- something that would please his parents and perhaps even make him a hero in their eyes. He did manage to graduate and find a job with a respected architectural firm, but it was at this time that he also was introduced to Quaaludes. To his joy, the effects of Quaaludes made the real world seem even more tolerable, less painful, and very far away -- like something you read about in the newspaper. Then one day, the wall that he had built between himself and the real world came crashing down on him. When he awoke, he was in the hospital. He felt terrible and it was the first time that he had noticed a vibration that seemed to pulse through his entire body. The physician told him that he had suffered two grand mal seizures while at work, he had lost consciousness, and had been brought to the hospital. Upon hearing this, the vibration grew more intense, but he said nothing. The doctor's words meant that he should give up one of his best friends--Quaaludes. He was struck by a sickening fear, not the fear of more seizures, or failing health, but the fear of giving up something that was so precious to him. To him, it was worse than the death of his parents or a family member. He would feel alone again, the mind-killing fear would return, and he knew he would become a social outcast again. He couldn't bare it. He couldn't talk to the doctor, all he wanted to do was get out of there. Upon his release from the hospital, he returned to the safe arms of his only true friend--Quaaludes. As his friend bathed his brain in the blue mist of escapism, his body was starting to react again. Soon the seizures came again along with the same medical warnings to stop. Although his mind was consumed with grief over the prospect of losing the only thing that gave his life purpose, security and meaning, he knew that not to heed the warnings meant permanent disability or even death. As always, the decision had been made for him by an all consuming and over powering outside world -- a world that he and his now dying best friend had held-off together for years. The vibration in his body became more intense.

The need for therapy was staring him in the face. He was overwhelmed by the recommendations that he received for this treatment program or that. Everyone seemed to know about the "magic bullet" treatment program that had the "right cure" and would set him free once again. The truth was that he didn't want a "magic bullet" shot into him, he didn't want to be set free. He had been happy doing what he was doing and he didn't want to change. He was living the big lie, and he liked it.

Yet he knew that he had to do something, so he tried several treatment plans. They were long term and slow, and none of them seemed to meet his individual needs. He was suffering and no one seemed to understand. He needed someone to connect with and to understand his pain, his desires, his fears, and his withdrawal. His mind and body were casting off the effects of the Quaaludes, but oh, how he longed to have them back. His journey seemed endless and aimless. He knew that his doctors were on the wrong path and the support groups that he had been sent to were also based on religious concepts that he felt that he was going to church. He wanted to be treated like a unique individual and it was at this point that he realized that one size did not fit all, and his internal vibration grew worse.

One day in therapy something wonderful happened. He now thinks of it as his awakening. The therapist suggested that he return to school -- he even called him "a quick and intelligent young man" -- can you imagine that, "a quick and intelligent young man." Those words rang in his ears for days to come. The therapist suggested that he become a part of youth counseling for young people having problems with drugs and alcohol. The idea struck him like thunder. Nothing had appealed to him more in years. He did return to school, a very motivated young man. His grades for the first time were excellent, he even surprised himself. He landed a job counseling at the YMCA and it opened new doors for him overnight. Suddenly he was confronted with people just like himself. People with similar backgrounds, similar fears, the same inadequacies, the same loneliness, and the same bad "friends" and bad habits. He was motivated to go back to graduate school and develop an entire new career for himself, a career where he could constantly help others out of the abyss and into the sunlight; thereby, avoiding the long, hard journey that he had taken.

After graduating and attaining his Ph.D. in Psychology, he realized that he held a unique position. He had understanding and empathy for those walking a similar pathway. He knew that life was good on its own merits and did not need to be masked and exiled just to cope on a daily basis. His psychological models, systems and procedures work -- offering hope to the hopeless, and bringing light to the darkness. Best of all, was that the internal vibration that had haunted him for so many years was finally gone. It had been replaced by confidence and a sense of knowing that his life was at last making a difference for the positive.

Of course, this is the story of the author, Marc Frederick Kern. He has been generous enough to share his very private story with us. It is important to him that you, the reader, realize that he has complete empathy for your life situation. He knows that simply by reading this far into this book, either you or someone you care about is experiencing deep personal difficulties at this time. His book is a product of his extensive training and personal experiences as a practicing Clinical Psychologist. Now is the time to put your trust in someone who cares, someone who knows, and someone who has been there and back. Let his book be the guidepost that leads you onto the pathway back to a satisfying and fulfilling life.

TAKE CONTROL NOW!

SPECIAL NOTE

THE PSYCHOLOGY OF CHANGE

- The main text of this book was created in the first person as a dialogue between you, the reader, and me, the psychotherapist, coach, and author. It is my intent to make this a meaningful, personal, and most importantly, a useful guide book to taking control of your life and developing the keys to healthy habits.

- This is a general book to help you make behavioral changes.

- Certain parts of this book discuss some of the traditional and best known addictions; however, this is a book on how to control or change ANY behavior deemed to be unhealthy. The addictions are only representative of some of the most important unhealthy habits, and the most difficult to change, and are not the primary focus of this book.

- This is a book on 'Taking Control' of your behavior by teaching you the basic principles of how we (Human Beings) mentally work. You will learn how to take control of what you can change, and learn how to feel in control of what you cannot change.

- Habits are never forgotten, the goal is to find a new habit that is healthy and eventually preferred, or becomes the new norm over the old norm.

- Taking control is not the same as willpower. The tools and the keys in this book are insights to getting around the pressure that willpowering creates, no matter what behavior you want to change.

- Willpower can also create a 'rubber band' effect. Your willpower can force a change to occur; however, when your willpower weakens, like a tightly stretched rubberband, you will snap back into your old behavior or old habit.

- The ideas and suggestions in this book are intended to supplement, not replace, the medical advice of a trained health care professional. All matters regarding your health require medical supervision. Consult a trained health care professional before adopting the suggestions in this book.

- In making any behavioral change it is important to remember that you should: "Skill Yourself, Don't Kill Yourself!"

TAKE CONTROL NOW!

CHAPTER 1   OVERCOMING YOUR OBJECTIONS

PART 1 THE SEDUCTIVENESS OF BAD HABITS

"It was the best of times, it was the worst of times, it was the age of wisdom, it was the age of foolishness, it was the epoch of belief, it was the epoch of incredulity, it was the season of light, it was the season of darkness, it was the spring of hope, it was the winter of darkness, we had everything before us, we had nothing before us, we were all going direct to Heaven, we were all going direct the other way--" This quote begins Charles Dickens' famous novel, "A Tale of Two Cities." However, it could also describe how you feel about your life or the life of someone important to you. These opposing feelings perfectly capture the emotions felt by so many people today. It can be the best of times in so many ways but it all can be destroyed by powerful and all-consuming bad habits. It can be a wonderful time of light and hope, only to be blackened by the darkness of despair caused by overwhelming unhealthy behavior habits. By practicing unhealthy lifestyle management habits either you or someone you love has gotten into a difficult and unpleasant place in life. This could center around one bad habit or a series of bad habits which include: smoking tobacco or marijuana, poor stress reduction skills, overeating, compulsive shopping, addictive depression, being a workaholic, constant self doubting, free-floating fear and anxiety, drinking too much on a regular basis, not following your doctor's advice, procrastination, misuse of prescription medication, lack of exercise, use of street drugs, poor work habits, hypochondria, poor study habits, consistent laziness, addiction to television, being a couch potato, gambling too much, sexual harassment, the compulsive use of pornography, and on and on. There are two types of unhealthy habits: the "YES" bad habits and the "NOT" bad habits. Both types are motivated by avoidance of uncomfortable feelings. However, type one is learned because of the feelings the habit or behavior itself offers. Type two evolves out of the feelings that an alternative non bad habit behavior offers. Both types reflect the resistance to give up that which is familiar, comfortable and predictable.

For example, type one--drugs, alcohol, gambling, procrastination, smoking, anger and the other addictions. Healthy habits are achieved by giving up the bad habit itself and replacing it with a number of healthy habits that must eventually become more rewarding than the bad habit.

Type two -- not taking medication, not following doctor's advice, not exercising, not eating the correct foods, not achieving, not studying, and poor work habits. Healthy habits are achieved in two steps; first, by giving up that which has been in its place (ie: sitting on the couch, not wanting to give up a lifestyle activity or inactivity, or not wanting to give up a taste, not wanting to give up a feeling, not wanting to give up a pleasure). Secondly, replacing the old habits with a number of new habits that become the new norm which is more rewarding than the old unhealthy habits.

These are all silent killers and are our own personally constructed devils which plague us and cut out pieces of our lives day-by-day. They also shorten and diminish the enjoyment of our life spans.

All of this type of unhealthy behavior forces us to say "Why me?!" -- "How did this happen to me?" -- "I don't deserve this!" Just as you read in my story at the beginning of this book, these unhealthy habits are a direct result of an intertwining of sociological, biological, and psychological events. It is both an adaptive and adoptive process.

It is important to look at this concept more closely. We didn't consciously choose to become addicted to a substance or a behavior. No one plans to become a prisoner of their own device in a cell of unhealthy behavior, but it happens every day. It is a subtle and seductive process which occurs over the course of time. What seems to happen is this: In the early stages of our unhealthy behavior, we are sociologically introduced to a substance or an activity that gives us immediate positive feelings while masking the realities and responsibilities of everyday life. Through friends, acquaintances, advertising, or just plain accident, we are introduced to things like cigarettes, alcohol, street drugs, pornography, shopping, the advantages of being sick, certain types of food, or even the 'good old' work ethic. Through the gradual use of these substances or behavior patterns our biological drives take over and we start to need or even crave this stimulus. Before we know it, the needs of our mind have taken control and through our psychological processes we can feel stimulated and relaxed at the same time. We can feel powerful and friendly, or closeted and protected from the world. It is the FEELING that leads to the ACTION. The substance or behavior that seems to work the best becomes our "Elixir" of choice, our "secret thing" that we do that we think no one else recognizes in us. Over time there becomes a secret person within you, a "you that nobody knows." Soon, 'our Elixir'--'our Secret' becomes a primary solution to many of our problems. Then suddenly, it becomes the dominant motivating force in our lives and transforms itself into more of a problem than the original problems that we were trying to escape.

HOW DID A SOLUTION BECOME A PROBLEM?

It quite simply was an adaptive and adoptive process. First we adapted to the habit and then we adopted it as part of our personality and as part of our need structure.

An easily understood example of how an adaptation might take place can be found in the use of a common over-the-counter product. Steven, a college freshman away from home for the first time, developed a severe cold just before a big exam. Anxious not to be slowed down, he went to a campus drug store and loaded up on non-prescription remedies, including nasal spray. He felt proud of himself for taking care of the problem without needing to call home to Mom for help. After a few sprays he was breathing easily and feeling dramatically better. In about a week his cold was gone, but he found himself still using the nose spray because he couldn't breathe comfortably without it.

What happened was a case of biological "rebound" -- a type of adaptation. It was as if Steven's body said: "Why should I produce the chemicals to keep my nose open when this spray works so well?" By using the spray, he had changed his body's own chemical manufacturing plant. The more his nose closed, the more he sprayed, and on and on. In a short time, he had created his own biological addiction. Soon, he was using the spray ten to twelve times a day, constantly increasing the dosage to achieve the same effect that he originally received from a single spray. But most importantly, if he didn't use the spray, he could not breathe comfortably at all, thereby, creating a greater problem than he had in the beginning.

In a similar process, many of us become addicted to sleeping medications, tranquilizers, and a multitude of over-the-counter drugs. Perhaps we initially suffer from insomnia for a valid reason. However, every time we take something, the part of our brain which produces sleep chemicals shuts down a bit, and then still more, until eventually our brain's chemical plant grinds to a slow halt. By choosing a chemical solution to a simple problem, this subtle undermining of the body begins to create a growing physical need, and

12

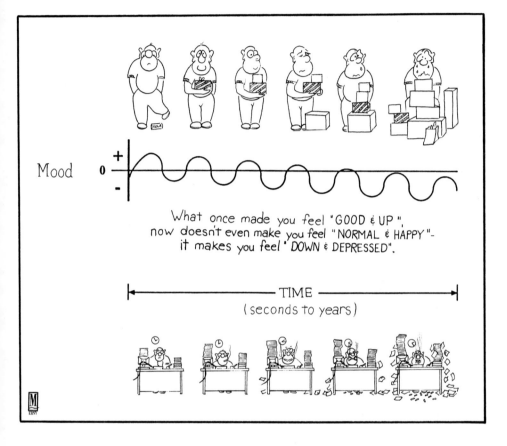

Mood

What once made you feel "GOOD & UP",
now doesn't even make you feel "NORMAL & HAPPY"-
it makes you feel "DOWN & DEPRESSED".

TIME
(seconds to years)

the beginnings of addiction take place. This is adaptation gone wrong, a self-created problem stemming from pure and simple innocence and naivete.

These biological adaptation processes are known as the "rebound and tolerance" effect. A psychological term for this reaction is called 'Tissue Hunger.' This causes us to feel unnatural without the usage of the substance. In short, our body becomes accustomed to the intoxicant and it needs more and more to register the desired, or same sensations.

What goes up must come down. What happens in all addictions and thrill-seeking activities and behavior is that for every high there is an equal, or even greater, opposite low.

Whether you are drinking, smoking cigarettes, eating certain foods, reading pornography, working too much, exercising too much, or even shopping too much; eventually the effect wears off, and you feel more depressed and un-fulfilled than before you participated in the activity. These shortcut solutions, once thought by the consumer to resolve certain uncomfortable emotions, in reality, only create more.

Psychological adaption works in much the same way as biological adaptation-- involving a coping response that goes off-track. There are a variety of ways to change our feelings, ranging from healthy habit tactics such as a game of tennis to the unhealthy quick-fix of eating to avoid boredom. Basically, the only difference between creating healthy habits and unhealthy addictions is the length of time they take to work. Healthy methods such as sports, exercise and constructive hobbies do more than just alter mood; they address underlying problems. The only trouble is they require time to take effect, while shortcuts, such as eating, drinking or spending assure immediate satisfaction.

A perfect example of this is the fourteen year old boy sitting in his living room alone and bored. So, he decides to try a bottle of his parent's beer. Suddenly, he discovers he is no longer restless. He feels stimulated, happy, and insulated from the bad feelings of real life. What he has discovered is a very powerful and falsely rewarding behavior pattern. He has learned that whenever he feels bored, alone, threatened, or restless, he can choose this particular shortcut and, just like pressing a button, the unwelcome sensation will magically be gone.

It is very important to mention at this time, that when most of us develop unhealthy lifestyle management habits we are generally going through a phase of life when we are striving to find ourselves as we develop self-identity and coping skills. If and when we discover these magical Elixirs, we suddenly have the illusion of control and mastery over our feelings. Unfortunately, this is an illusion. It is unfounded and it is dangerously deceptive.

The fourteen year old boy, after taking a drink or two, now feels grown-up, INDEPENDENT, and less in need of parental or peer approval. What happens, over the course of time, is that he learns that these shortcut solutions--whether it is the use of food, drugs, or thrill-seeking activities--do work. They don't just work in one area of life, but in many. Eventually, he discovers more shortcuts for dealing with unpleasant feelings, and these replace authentic methods for coping. Over time, the shortcuts are used to get rid of boredom, stress, loneliness, anger, and anxiety. They seem to increase happiness and sociability while reducing guilt feelings and compensate for low self-esteem.

This is why we resist change. We are afraid of giving up our unhealthy behavior habits because it means letting go of the only things which always work in our lives that make us feel good. Anything else such as tennis, music, or a social life have been replaced and phased out until they no longer work for us. New ways of coping have never been developed in our lives because real coping takes a lot longer and works less predictably than chemical or thrill-producing activities. The feelings that appear after stopping unhealthy lifestyle habits have always been there, but were masked by the short-cut solutions of intoxicants or behaviors, and now we have to cope with the discomforts of normal life.

Dr. Stanton Peele, author of "Love and Addiction," has developed another useful concept of psychological adaptation. According to his theory, people become addicted not just to a particular substance or activity, but to the total experience which that habit provides. When we become familiar with a certain way of life--even when that "something" is extremely negative (such as an abusive relationship), we tend to settle into a familiar comfort zone. We see frequent evidence of this phenomenon when abused children grow up and repeatedly select adult relationships similar to those in their past.

People frequently wonder why battered wives refuse to press charges against the spouse who put them in the hospital, and then dismiss the battered wife with the old cliche, "She could leave if she wanted to." But it isn't that easy. When we remove ourselves from even the most destructive situations -- if these scenarios have become natural and normal to us -- we are faced with a sense of overwhelming loss. And in most cases, without competent intervention, that vacuum causes us to continue to choose known sorrows rather than unknown alternatives.

I have personally noted that most of the clients that I work with in my practice tell me that when they stop their unhealthy behavior activities, they simply don't know what to do with themselves, especially in the evenings. They often relapse because of this painful vacuum. For example, I know a person who complains that if she stops overeating, she won't know what to do with her time. Not that she eats all the time, but it is always on her mind -- planning the next snack and the next meal. She has expressed fear at the thought

Psychological Adaptation — "Taking the shortcuts of life causes you to unlearn . . . "

of what she will do at parties; how she will handle romantic advances and so on. As upset as she is by weight gain, it is, at least, familiar territory. It is familiar and, therefore, comfortable, non-threatening and safe.

The reverse side of this is that if we have been doing something for a long time, we don't always realize what we are really doing. For example, a man came in to see me regarding his unhealthy habit of smoking cigarettes. He said that for years his family, friends and doctor have been telling him to stop because of a persistent cough. He said, "For years people commented on my coughing, but I didn't believe I coughed that much until one day, I was in the room with my pet parrot, and instead of talking and saying cute things he was copying my coughing! What a shock. I realized that I had to have coughed hundreds of times around the bird for him to reproduce the sound so perfectly." The fact is, you may be doing hundreds of small but destructive things every day and not realize it because you have been doing them so long. They don't stand out in your mind and, therefore, they are unrecognizable to you.

There are social or sociological, as well as, biological and psychological adaptations. These social adaptations cause us to become first lured and then trapped in unhealthy behavior. When we begin taking shortcuts to handle life's discomforts it is all too easy to build a lifestyle around our addictions. If we feel guilty about eating or drinking too much, the typical strategy is to start spending more time with people who enjoy rather than criticize our habits. We find ourselves withdrawing from the community that makes us conscious of our unhealthy behavior. If we are into gambling, drinking, or shopping we tend to build our friendships in these areas. We, in essence, are building support groups that give validity to our unhealthy lifestyle. After a while, activities and acquaintances unrelated to our habit lose their importance and may even become a source of annoyance. As we distance ourselves from the normal life, what most people consider to be normal now becomes unfamiliar, uncomfortable, and even unacceptable to us. To return to a normal life, you would need to make radical adjustments in order to compensate for your acclamation to life on the edge. It would be far easier had you never used shortcuts in the first place. To paraphrase the old cliche: "You've made your bed and now you find yourself sleeping in it." ISN'T IT TIME TO GET OUT OF BED?!

With this important background information in your mind, IT IS VERY IMPORTANT THAT YOU DO NOT FEEL BAD ABOUT YOURSELF! You must realize that you never intended to become entangled by these habits. You never sat down one day and deliberately and consciously decided that unhealthy lifestyle habits would dominate and control your life. As we have just discussed, it has been an intertwining of sociological introduction to bad habits, developed biological cravings, and a creation of psychological needs that have brought you to where you are now. On the surface unhealthy lifestyle activities look very attractive and alluring. It is only after you have become entangled in their web that you realize how destructive they really are. There is an old saying that states: "On the surface evil looks attractive." This is true, no one is attracted to something that is obviously ugly and repugnant on the surface. We are drawn to things that look attractive and pleasant. Frequently, we discover that ugliness and discomfort exists only after we are deeply involved in an activity that on the surface looked wonderful.

Now is the time to decide to make a change. Now is the time to decide to conquer any habit, behavior, belief, or chemical that is unhealthy or dangerous for you. Now is the time to take control and do something that makes sense. Now is the time to grow, and now

HOW ARE YOU DOING ?

Rate how satisfied you are presently with the following areas of your life:

-10	-5	0	5	10
Very Dissatisfied	Somewhat Dissatisfied	Neutral	Somewhat Satisfied	Very Satisfied

Career/Employment......................................	-10	-5	0	5	10
Friends/Companionship.............................	-10	-5	0	5	10
Family..	-10	-5	0	5	10
Leisure Activities/Hobbies..........................	-10	-5	0	5	10
Intimate Relationships...............................	-10	-5	0	5	10
Drug or Alcohol Use/Cravings	-10	-5	0	5	10
Unhealthy Habit/Cravings	-10	-5	0	5	10
Eating Behavior/Cravings...........................	-10	-5	0	5	10
Self-Esteem	-10	-5	0	5	10
Physical Health	-10	-5	0	5	10
Psychological Well-Being...........................	-10	-5	0	5	10
Sexual Fulfillment	-10	-5	0	5	10
Spiritual Well-Being..................................	-10	-5	0	5	10

is the time to make a positive difference in your life. Make the commitment to yourself, don't feel bad about yourself, or feel sorry for yourself. Instead, have the courage, strength, and desire to read on. It is the purpose of this book to help you untangle yourself in a do-able, easy-to-understand way.

At this point, you need to pause for a moment and complete the "HOW ARE YOU DOING?" chart. This is an important tool that you will use again as a measure from which to evaluate the change made from reading this book. It is an easy chart to use. As you will see there is a scale at the top ranging from a -10 to a +10. Minus 10 means very unsatisfied graduating to a plus 10 which means very satisfied. There is a list on topics running from top to bottom along the left-hand side of the page. Think carefully about how you feel about each topic. For example, the first topic is your Career. You have choices that grade your satisfaction rate as being 'very dissatisfied' - 'somewhat dissatisfied' - 'neutral-or no feeling about the topic' - 'somewhat satisfied' - and 'very satisfied.' Simply circle the rating that most closely matches your feelings about your career at this time. Then proceed to do the same with the remainder of the topics. After you have completed the chart, please continue with the book.

Now that you have an assessment of your current life in your mind, and now that you have decided to make a change in your life, the most important thing to do is have the resolve to carry it out! It is easy to make excuses and to lie to yourself. You will find that ambivalence will become your worst enemy. You will find yourself "sitting on the fence" saying things like: "I want to stop drinking but . . . " Or "I can't lose weight until . . . " Such statements spotlight those mixed emotions which are the thieves that undermine all your efforts. It's important to understand that it is natural to have feelings that are on both sides of the fence. If drinking is negatively affecting your job, relationships, or health, there are still compelling payoffs for you, or you wouldn't continue drinking. In many significant ways your life is going to be better without alcohol, but that doesn't erase the fact that you are going to miss the kick of unwinding on Friday nights or enhancing a meal with a bottle of wine. Another example would be that even though you may enjoy wearing small sizes in clothing, and you think that you look better at a lighter weight, you realize that it is going to be very unpleasant giving up the satisfaction that rich desserts give you.

Ambivalence is much like a teeter-totter on a child's playground. Middle ground, that perfect balance, is rarely achieved and is more often the reason that we cannot muster the energy to change. Often we keep waiting for clearer readings, a bold tipping to one side or the other, that will propel us into that change.

It is extremely important that we acknowledge the rewarding aspects of our habitual unhealthy behaviors. Drinking, for example, might provide you with the courage to ask someone to dance, or it might help you combat stress, loneliness, depression, or help you to bring on sleep. It is imperative that you recognize the rewards you reap from your destructive activity. The cost/benefit ratio is both an intellectual and emotional assessment, and this knowledge can be used to provide direct insight into skill deficit areas.

Along with ambivalence there are certain enticing mood states which originate with bad habits. An example might be the alcohol user who feels that under the influence, he reaches a state of euphoria otherwise unobtainable from any other source. Given this, it's understandable that he might feel he's losing a "good friend." The same emotions apply to alcohol, cigarettes, food, salt, sugar, compulsive shopping, excessive exercise, etc. You

Sitting on the fence reflects your
ambivalence – accept it!

must realize that even when you've learned to replace these pleasures with other rewards, you may always feel a certain sense of loss or nostalgia on some level.

As in many phases of life, ambivalence tends to ebb and flow like the tide. As you waffle back and forth, you'll need to develop 'sea legs' to help weather the changing tides of emotion. When you learn to 'roll' comfortably with these shifts in feeling and motivation, you will have the best chance of making a permanent lifestyle change. Remember, permanent resolve is your primary direction and one of your primary keys. You must truly work toward making the decision in your conscious mind that you are going to develop healthy habits. You must train yourself to not lie to yourself by making unreasonable excuses for postponement of your primary goal. Do not allow your subconscious to come to the fore and attack the reasoned logic of your primary goal. Keep your strength and your resolve. Be true to your healthy intentions, be persistent, work on healthy activities that make you feel better in the long run.

Let's look at Ambivalence vs. Denial. In my clinical work, I have found that the concept of ambivalence is much more honest and helpful than that of denial. It is my belief that few people are really in denial about their problem, they do recognize the problem and are aware of it's difficulties. Instead, I believe that people are ambivalent -- sitting on the fence -- about the prospect of all that work, all that change, all those feelings to deal with. It's easy for an outsider to see the high cost of excessive unhealthy behavior such as over eating, over drinking, drug use, over spending, hypochondria, etc. It is possible that they may wonder aloud, "Why does he/she do that to himself/herself?" "Why not just say no and stop?"

The problem is that these people are looking at only one side of the teeter-totter. They would have to be inside the skin of the other person in order to understand the complex relationship. A person has to deal within himself and the overwhelming ambivalence that accompanies it. If you or someone you love is involved in a destructive habit, you can reason that he/she is ambivalent; that there are deeply rooted personal pro's and con's which affect all of his/her actions. While such behavior may not appear to be rational to others, it makes ironic but perfect sense to any person who has ever been the captive of an overpowering unhealthy behavior.

Ambivalence is a very tricky thing, especially when you have been engaging in your unhealthy habit for a long period of time. If the ambivalence would only go away, it would be much easier to have the resolve to give up the unwanted behavior. The truth is, that ambivalence may never completely go away. Years from now, you may suddenly have a yearning for the unhealthy habit that you gave up. Ambivalence is normal, and I believe that it is healthy, and that we are stronger individuals the longer we accept that ambivalence is there and work with it.

I have included a chart to help you explore and accept the exact nature of your own ambivalence. Fill it out as completely and honestly as possible and keep it on your refrigerator door or bathroom medicine cabinet, as a reminder of your mixed thoughts and feelings about the changes you are trying to make. Remember, these thoughts and feelings are normal, but need to be faced and dealt with. It may take a long time to acknowledge everything in this chart, so work on it and add to it, as new thoughts and feelings arise.

Take the "Accepting My Ambivalence Chart" and make a list of the positives and negatives of stopping or getting control over an unhealthy habit. I have made partial lists of

ACCEPTING MY AMBIVALENCE
ABOUT MY ___OVEREATING___ HABIT

The Positives I get from continuing this habit.	The Positives I get from stopping this habit.
1. I CAN STILL ENJOY MY FAVORITE FOODS.	1. MY HEALTH WILL IMPROVE.
2. I WON'T FEEL DEPRIVED.	2. I WILL HAVE MORE ENERGY.
3. I WON'T GET CRANKY/IRRITABLE.	3. MY APPEARANCE WILL BE BETTER.
4. I'LL HAVE THE "REWARD" I WANT AT THE END OF THE DAY.	4. I CAN WEAR CLOTHES FROM ANY SHOP OR DEPT. STORE.
5. I WON'T HAVE TO COMPETE IN THE DATING SCENE.	5. I WILL FEEL BETTER ABOUT MYSELF.
6. I'LL HAVE AN EXCUSE FOR BEING REJECTED BY OTHERS.	6. I WILL FACE LESS PREJUDICE AND DISCRIMINATION.
7.	7.
8.	8.
9.	9.
10.	10.
The Negatives I get from continuing this habit.	**The Negatives I get from stopping this habit.**
1. MY SOCIAL LIFE WILL REMAIN LIMITED.	1. I WON'T BE ABLE TO GO TO MY FAVORITE FAST FOOD RESTAURANT ANYMORE.
2. MY HEALTH WILL SUFFER.	2. PEOPLE WILL EXPECT MORE OF ME IF I ACCOMPLISH THIS WEIGHT LOSS.
3. MY APPEARANCE WILL REMAIN POOR.	3. I'LL HAVE TO SPEND A LOT OF MONEY ON NEW CLOTHES THAT FIT.
4. I MAY FIND THAT JOB OPPORTUNITIES ARE LIMITED BECAUSE OF DISCRIMINATION.	4. I'LL HAVE TO COMPETE SOCIALLY, JUST LIKE EVERYONE ELSE DOES.
5. I WILL BE PERCEIVED BY OTHERS POORLY.	5. I'LL HAVE TROUBLE RELAXING IF I CAN'T EAT WHAT I WANT.
6. I'LL NEVER WANT TO BUY NEW CLOTHES.	6. PEOPLE OF THE OPPOSITE SEX WILL APPROACH ME FOR DATES.
7.	7.
8.	8.
9.	9.
10.	10.

ACCEPTING MY AMBIVALENCE ABOUT MY _____ HABIT

The Positives I get from continuing this habit.	The Positives I get from stopping this habit.
1._____	1._____
2._____	2._____
3._____	3._____
4._____	4._____
5._____	5._____
6._____	6._____
7._____	7._____
8._____	8._____
9._____	9._____
10._____	10._____

The Negatives I get from continuing this habit.	The Negatives I get from stopping this habit.
1._____	1._____
2._____	2._____
3._____	3._____
4._____	4._____
5._____	5._____
6._____	6._____
7._____	7._____
8._____	8._____
9._____	9._____
10._____	10._____

some of the most common positive and negative reasons in the categories of Overeating and Drinking Too Much. Remember, this is only a partial list in the two categories of unhealthy habits that I have compiled in order to get you thinking about your own reasons. Read them use them, and add to them.

Now, make a contract with yourself. Take the Ambivalence Chart that you have just completed and turn it over. List all the excuses that you might give yourself or someone else for not giving up your bad habit. Think carefully about it and be sure to list them all. Excuses such as:

- I'm too tired.

- I'll start tomorrow.

- It's really not that bad.

- It's too hard.

- I just want to do it one more time.

- I really wasn't doing it for myself.

- I don't want to feel out of control.

- I'm too old to change.

- It will be easier after the holiday season or the new year.

- I'll wait until my husband/wife is more supportive.

- I'll start after things settle down at the office, and the work pressure eases-up.

Continue on and on with your excuses. After you have completed all the excuses you can think of, write the following on the bottom of the page: I WILL NOT USE ANY OF THE ABOVE EXCUSES, UNDER ANY CIRCUMSTANCES! Now, sign it and date it. Put it in plain sight somewhere where everyone can see it and so you can use it every day.

Isn't it time to do it now?!

Your next challenge is coping with other people's ambivalence about your change. There is an old saying that: "No man is an island unto himself." As children we have heard this on many occasions but probably didn't understand it. It simply means that we humans do not and cannot live isolated or separate lives. We live in communities that are all interconnected in some way. If our spouse, child, parent, friend, colleague or roommate experiences a crisis or misfortune, it affects our life in some way and to some degree.

In essence, you have not been alone with your bad habit. Even if your family and friends have been nagging you to lose weight, stop drinking, stop smoking tobacco or marijuana, reduce the use of salt or sugar, etc., there has evolved over time a coalition of sorts between you and everyone with whom you interact regularly. That means that the people in your life are familiar, if not happy with, the way things have been. So, when you begin to make changes, you are asking them to change too. Since they are changing along with you, they may experience ambivalence of their own. Anyone who decides to make serious lifestyle changes must assume that there will be considerable interfering social forces with which to contend. You must become assertive and independent if you are to be successful. I assure you that your true inner self will remain intact and it will be a happier 'you' when you reach your new healthier destination.

I have helped hundreds of people through successful life transformations. As you venture down this road of change, you will come to a thousand and one forks in the road. Each time you have a choice, you can take the old path or the new one. If you decide to take the new path and find it rewarding, you will want to continue. If you don't like it, all you have to do is back-track a little, wait for a while at your last point of progress, and then continue once again down the new path with renewed resolve to succeed. It is you, and you alone, that will always be in complete control of choosing the changes that you make and keep in your life. The person that you become at the end of this journey will be very definitely you. You will be happier and more powerful because you have made all the choices yourself and at your own speed. Perhaps for the first time ever in your life you will not be a victim of your past history and biology but a creation of your own choosing.

Ambivalence is such a basic part of our make-up that we experience it to some degree in most aspects of our lives. It must be accepted as a part of life. Don't allow your mixed feelings about changing your unhealthy habit to interfere with your progress. You have the understanding to overcome all of your objections simply by using the tools that have just been outlined. Start to work now, in spite of your "fence sitting" attitudes.

Remember, in order to take control: "Skill Yourself, Don't Kill Yourself!"

TAKE CONTROL NOW!

CHAPTER 1 OVERCOMING YOUR OBJECTIONS

PART 2 YOUR FEELINGS AND THE INTERNAL POINT OF CONTROL

As we learned from the exercises and text in Part One of this chapter, our slogan should be, "Don't kill yourself, skill yourself." Instead of just 'getting along by going along,' you have to ask yourself: "What am I going to trade my life for?" "Am I going to trade all my shining possibilities for the dim, cave-like existence of unhealthy habits?" Am I going to stop blaming my failure on others and set my vision on becoming a renewed, happier, competent person who is in control of my life and is able to manage my feelings?" Your vision acts like a rope that is stretched across the river so that you can hold on when the waters get rough and you want to give up, when your old feelings become almost too powerful to manage.

We humans pride ourselves as being the "thinking" beings on this planet. In reality, even for us, everything starts as a feeling. I firmly believe that emotions, more than thoughts, motivate our actions. Thoughts cause us to have different feelings, but it is that feeling that actually results in the way we behave. As I stated, we like to claim that we are intellectual beings, while in truth, we are primarily creatures of emotion and feelings. For example, if it weren't for the existence of positive feelings accompanying a goal, most people would not pursue activities involving delayed gratification, such as getting an advanced educational degree or getting married. Motivation in life is simply a matter of moving TOWARD a feeling or AWAY from a feeling. All behavior is basically the result of "payoffs" (a feeling or state that usually makes you feel better than you did) which result from a certain action or behavior.

There is a basic equation which I have developed called F-A-N which sums this up so that it is easy to understand. It is the basic motivational relationship of life and everything that we do. F+A=N, stands for F [feelings] + A [actions] = N [new feelings]. Actions that bring about a desired new feeling will tend to be repeated while those that result in an undesirable feeling are not likely to become habitual. At times we engage in a particular behavior in hope of finding a new feeling or pleasurable sensation. In developing healthy habits, the positive rewards come after the activity or behavior. For example, weight lifting is very strenuous, and a lot of unpleasant work, but it results in a very positive effect on your weight and physique. The unpleasantness comes first and the reward comes second. While drinking alcohol produces pleasant effects in the beginning by giving a person a euphoric feeling and by blurring the reality of life, it is followed by the very negative effects of the 'hang-over' which produces a headache, body bloating, weight gain, and sometimes, nausea. To repeat, good or healthy habits works with negative feelings up front, followed by the reward or the positive feelings (good/healthy habit=first -, secondly +). The bad or unhealthy habit begins with feelings that are pleasant followed by very bad feelings (bad/unhealthy habit=first +, secondly -).

Keep in mind that any activity or substance capable of changing your feelings, can and will motivate and prompt a variety of behaviors, and therefore has great influence over you (be it healthy or unhealthy behavior). Remember, it is easy to be seduced into unhealthy habits; however, it is not your fault since you did not willingly choose them. There is no shame and no blame.

As I have stated, no one chooses to become reliant on substances or behavior patterns. No one strives to become an excessive drinker, a workaholic, a compulsive

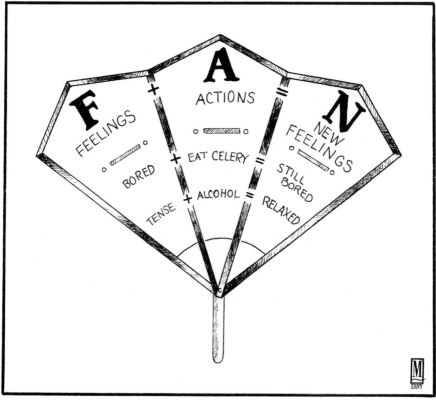

The Foundation of Change

shopper, an overeater, a couch potato, a procrastinator, a street drug user, or a compulsive gambler. Instead, we get caught in these behaviors and activities because we lack self-awareness and knowledge about the nature of the substance we are using or the behavior in which we are engaged. Without an understanding of our emotions and what it is we are trying to avoid or achieve, breaking a bad habit is virtually impossible.

At this point in the book, I would like to insert a personal message to you. In my individual journey to the development of healthy habits, I was under the care of many well-meaning doctors and therapists. Frequently, I got 'off track' by trying to give them complete control. In essence, I wanted to use the "short-cut life" approach again by putting all the responsiblilty for me on their shoulders, and I would just go along for the ride and make myself dependent again, this time on them. This delayed the formulation of my own new healthy lifestyle management habits that were beneficial for me personally. The extreme frustration of experiencing delay upon delay, and taking pathway after pathway, motivated me to embark on a new career in the field of Psychology, so that I could open new doors for others. It is important to me that others have a more structured and do-able plan than I had to follow.

While in school, my psychology professors taught me to develop or find a theory to guide my thinking and actions. This theory or model is the framework or basic road map, which remains open for change and correction, that explains the "whys," and which answers the questions. What I have explained so far in this chapter, and what will follow, is all part of a psychological model which I have created from my own experiences and education. It incorporates much wisdom from the self-help movement and the cutting edge of professional literature. It is designed to help you move forward, even when you don't feel like it. The exercises, charts, and text in this chapter can act as your anchor, and I hope that you read it not once, but several times until you feel comfortable with the tools and explanations presented in it. Remember, without a good foundation, it will be more difficult to use the tools that follow.

As you have just learned, after we have developed unhealthy lifestyle habits -- with the positive feelings delivered at the beginning of the activity and the negative feelings delivered at the end of the activity -- we soon discover that we continue to engage in our unhealthy habits not because we are looking for a good feeling anymore, but because we just don't want any worse feelings to come along. This is why it is so important to grasp this next concept.

If you are going to take control and make healthy lifestyle management changes that last, you must develop an Internal Locus (Point) of Control. Unless you want to be permanently dependent on outside forces to keep you 'on track,' you must look within yourself. You need to accept full responsibility for the desired healthy changes in order to become the dynamic center of your own life. This is what I did when I took the responsibility for myself off the shoulders of my doctors and therapists. When you do this, just as I did, you will develop the focal point for achieving your self-determined goals. While it is correct to acknowledge the presence of biological, sociological, and psychological influences, as we have already done, it is time for you to take ultimate responsibility for your life. You now need to become the one behind the wheel, in the driver's seat.

Although you are affected by predestined factors in the past, you can learn to compensate for them when you decide to take charge. Although I encourage you to interact

Stop fooling yourself about who really is in control.

with others and avail yourself of a variety of literature, in the end, you must become a self-correcting, self-asserting machine.

I realize that you have been in a destructive relationship with a particular unhealthy habit or behavior. As I have stated several times, the purpose of this book is to help pull you out of those negative patterns and enable you to develop constructive habits in their place. You are in the process of learning how to develop ever-increasing internal levels of control over your behavior by increasing the self responsibility of your entire life.

The Internal Locus (Point) of Control concept was developed by Rotter, the well-known psychologist. He was the first, on record, to notice that some individuals seem to be directed by thoughts and feelings emanating from within, while others appear to run their lives according to external forces -- like a leaf in the wind.

As comically illustrated by the fellow in the cartoon, the reason we engage in destructive habits is not due to external forces beyond our control. We can choose or not choose to walk into the ice cream parlor. We are not pulled, as the cartoon depicts, by some all-powerful mystical force. Even though it sometimes feels that we are forced to engage in our bad habits, in actuality, the 'pull' comes from within. The reason you veer off the highway toward your favorite bar, fast-food restaurant, or shopping mall is so that you can satisfy an internal need. It is this all-consuming need that you will learn to master. First, just accept the fact that this need comes from within, and stop wasting your time and energy looking for answers elsewhere.

It is useful to compare yourself to an explorer embarking on a voyage toward a compelling and rewarding destination. Think of yourself as a kind of Christopher Columbus character. As you begin this challenging voyage, your final destination is not in sight, but it

You can't see the end of your journey
from the safety of the dock.

is in your mind. You know where you want to go. As you move into uncharted waters, you may, from time to time, need to return to the shore or even the starting point to regroup, re-plan, and load-up on new supplies. The important thing is not to penalize or punish yourself when this happens. This is quite simply an expected part of your journey and adventure.

On your journey, whenever you find that a particular tactic is not proving effective, you must change your course. During these times you will need to admit to feeling pressure and feeling overwhelmed. Do not respond with despair or inactivity. Instead, admit and reaffirm that you must now take a new direction and continue with even greater effort and resolve.

If you find that a particular problem or habit is slowing your general progress, instead of using it as an excuse, gear-up to take definite steps to conquer it. If and when your effort doesn't produce the results you desire, you will have to pause, rethink the strategy and build the internal strength to start over again. This back and forth action is a normal part of your journey toward healthy lifestyle management habits.

The most important thing is to realize that 'If at first you don't succeed' -- once, twice, or even after many attempts, there is no reason to feel depressed, discouraged, or even embarrassed. This is quite normal. You cannot expect an approach to work the first few times out. If it does -- **Great!** If it doesn't, try something else or something more. Keep working and using your own creativity, and you will get it right!

Remember our slogan: "Don't Kill Yourself, Skill Yourself."

CHAPTER 1   OVERCOMING YOUR OBJECTIONS

PART 3   A LIFETIME TRAINING MANUAL FOR SELF-MANAGEMENT

What is offered here is a lifetime training manual for developing healthy life management skills. Externalizing responsibility, or blaming someone or something else for your problems, is something that we've all done and it simply does not work. You are going to have to take charge and take responsibility for yourself until you make it work.

I understand that dancing with anxiety, fear, pain, boredom and self-doubt is a major part of your life right now. You are listening to the constant chatter of the mind, those subconscious thoughts just below the surface, controlling awareness. These thoughts are confusing you, controlling you, and containing you. START TO CHANGE IT NOW!! Move in so close to that chatter of the mind, so close to that quick subconscious stream of thoughts that it scares you. Next, start to change it by focusing in on it and gently allow your powerful conscious thoughts to gently, very gently, bring the thought stream of the mind back into proper alignment. Begin to free yourself from those thoughts! After all, they are only thoughts -- nothing else.

At first, you must accept becoming more comfortable with the pain, anxiety and doubt. Then, as you gain more and more control of yourself, and the healing from within begins, these feelings and terrors will slowly fade away like a stain being bleached out of a tablecloth.

Your progress will come in many stages and there will be many plateaus. Just as Robert Goddard, the father of the modern day rocket engine learned; he certainly didn't just sit down, and draw a set of plans for a fuselage and an engine. Nor did he get it right after

41

a few tries. There were explosions and failures time after consecutive time. As each attempt failed and fizzled before him, he went back to the drawing board, often confused, frustrated, and afraid, and examined both the strengths and weaknesses of his latest failed set of plans. He would then make revisions from what he had learned, and try again and again and again. He built on what he knew worked for him, but most importantly, on what didn't.

You know, there is tremendous value in repetition, reflection and persistence because each repeated effort is another step up the ladder toward unlocking the secrets of ultimate success. So, let's agree together, right now, that there is no possibility of failure where your goals are concerned, only the continued advancement toward success!

I have noticed that most books that deal with behavior change usually state the need for definite goals. But, more often than not, they are goals that are too rigid and that interfere with getting the 'ball rolling' and maintaining momentum. In real life, goals are something we are always reaching for, but seldom attain. Goals are better looked upon as being guideposts, something to focus on, but certainly not an end in themselves. What's really important is for you to decide that you want to change the behavior in your life. Equally important, is that you feel good about it and that you are on the road toward achieving that reality.

The four essential goals that I suggest should act as guideposts for moving from unhealthy habits to developing healthy habits are:

1. Strive toward giving up dependent thinking and inaction.

2. Always strive toward reducing the harm caused by your habit.

3. Aim toward becoming comfortable with change and uncomfortable feelings.

4. Establish a new lifestyle that is more rewarding than the old. (Get a [new] life.)

The concept of 'dependent' isn't new or really that useful. However, it does convey a basic truth: that all people with unhealthy lifestyle management habits seem to be unaware of how their thinking and behaviors are dependent-oriented. Without exception, I have never worked with a person who didn't wish that someone else would develop a magic formula that would make his habit easier to break. I can't tell you how many groups/seminars/sessions I have conducted where people come to listen, and then go home and don't do anything with the information. They come back the following week and complain that nothing has changed. Most typically, they will say, "Dr. Kern, I need more tools and skills." I reply, "You have all the tools you need, just stop procrastinating and do what you know you need to do. Stop whining about how hard it is because no one is going to do it for you. The sooner you accept this, the sooner you'll be free of your unhealthy habits and in control of your life."

Of course, I realize this is easier said than done, especially when your whole life has been based on that kind of thinking. Changing behavior requires hard, persistent work. It is the same story -- the sooner you realize that there are no short-cuts, no magic pills, and no easy solutions, the sooner you will arrive at your destination. Stop looking around and asking "Why Me?' or, "Why do other people have it so easy?" It's up to you to break out of your prison of negative thinking. Don't hide yourself in a prison cell of self-imposed isolation. Mobilize yourself every day. You think that your habit is controlling you, but it is really your mind. Give thanks 365 days a year that you know where to look to find your way back home. You can conquer your habits, life can be like it was or even better than before you developed the habits. You CAN go home again. Like the Nike athletic shoe advertisements say: "JUST DO IT!"

43

Your next goal should be to focus on reducing the harmful effects of your habits. I will repeat, focus on reducing not just eliminating the harmful effects of your habit. Of course, this may result in you having to stop some activity or chemical use. Harm reduction simply means making the best of biological, psychological, and sociological factors which have and will continue to affect you. The only attainable goal here is to get involved in the process of making your habits less and less destructive. You should strive toward becoming comfortable while working toward your goal rather than obsessing about the end result. That 'perfect ending' probably will never come, at least not precisely the way you visualize it now. It is definitely not a requirement for a happy, healthy life. Your old goal of losing 30 pounds or never taking another drink again, or stopping compulsive shopping "cold turkey" may only work against you. You must shift your emphasis to the realistic goal of reducing the negative impacts of your habit by working toward a new lifestyle of self-exploration. You have been operating on a 'fantastic" level, now it is time to operate on a 'realistic' level.

This is important, so let me repeat it. Your new lifestyle must become your principal goal. In fact, the other three goals listed here are merely ways of accomplishing this. If you lose weight or stop using drugs, **GREAT!** However, those specific objectives should be secondary to your overall focus of creating a happy and healthy way of living the rest of your life. The process of change toward this new lifestyle needs to be your guiding focus. To succeed you will need to become comfortable and familiar with this new lifestyle, and if you start to let go, you must refocus and get back on track. In my years of working with all kinds of people, with all types of unhealthy habits, it is the ones who are able to acquire this strong focus who are able to eliminate or significantly reduce their bad habits on a long-term basis.

Finally, you must learn to enjoy the process of change and accept that it is all right to be comfortable with the change. As you begin to see some progress, your self-esteem will increase. But if you are focused on that final reward, you won't appreciate your achievements along the way. Change comes in small stages followed by long plateaus. The plateaus don't mean that you aren't changing. Enjoy the plateaus -- just "stop and smell the roses." Similarly, like a runner warming up, part of your task in making lifestyle changes involves getting emotionally limbered up. That means learning to feel comfortable with personal evolution, developing keener insights into self-control, self-responsibility, environmental awareness and the dynamic nature of change and growth.

The goal of change in any and all forms is the essential key. The moment you create even the simplest change, you have taken another step toward developing and attaining a new lifestyle.

I have included a worksheet that will help you at this stage entitled "GET A LIFE." As you will notice, I have prepared and inserted a hand-written example of how to use this worksheet, which is followed by blank worksheets for your use. You may find it helpful to photo copy the worksheets so they are more convenient to use. This is a very important exercise. Do not ignore it or skip it! Start to work on it immediately!

We must now move on to the interesting and important topic of ABSTINENCE VS. MODERATION. When someone first enters my care for treatment of habits that should be stopped altogether, one of the first questions I ask is, "Do you want to stop your habit entirely, or would you rather practice moderation?" With rare exception, I hear an immediate, "I sure would like to be able to smoke or drink occasionally, like other people." or "I wish I could learn to gamble/exercise/eat/shop moderately and less often, like normal

45

GET A LIFE !

Changing one unhealthy habit requires changing many lifestyle habits. To gain control of one part of your life requires you to develop a balanced overall life. This guide will help you identify areas of your life you need to change, identify the destination you want to achieve, develop steps to reach that destination, and push you to take control as soon as possible.

Subject/Habit	Where are you now?	Where would you like to be?	What steps do you need to take?	When?
Family	• NOT GETTING ALONG WITH MY PARENTS • POOR RELATIONSHIP WITH MY KIDS	• HAVE MY PARENTS BE PROUD OF ME • STRONG, LOVING RELATIONSHIP WITH MY CHILDREN	• STOP DOING DRUGS • GET A BETTER JOB • STOP HANGING AROUND WITH MY UNEMPLOYED FRIENDS	NOW!
Intimate Relationships	• NONE — I SPEND MOST OF MY TIME ALONE	• INVOLVED IN A ROMANTIC, HAPPY RELATIONSHIP	• STOP SPENDING MY EVENING HOURS ALONE & STONED • START GOING TO THE GYM AT NIGHT	TODAY!
Employment/ Career	• UNSATISFIED AND UNDER-PAID • NO CHANCE FOR PROMOTION • HATE GOING TO WORK EVERYDAY	• MAKING MORE MONEY • APPRECIATED & RESPECTED BY MY BOSS • GREATER CHANCE FOR PROMOTION	• SEND OUT RESUMES • TAKE NIGHT CLASSES • READ UP ON MY AREA OF INTEREST	YESTERDAY
Friendships	• NO TRUSTWORTHY FRIENDS	• HAVE FRIENDS I CAN CONFIDE IN & TRUST	• START ATTENDING CHURCH • MAKE AN EFFORT TO BUILD POSITIVE FRIENDSHIPS • HAVE LUNCH WITH CO-WORKERS	NOW!!

GET A LIFE !

Subject/Habit	Where are you now?	Where would you like to be?	What steps do you need to take?	When?
Social Life, Group Organizations	• ISOLATED & LONELY	• A PART OF THE GROUP — INCLUDED IN ACTIVITIES THAT ARE FUN	• JOIN A SOCIAL GROUP AT MY CHURCH • JOIN A SAILING CLUB	• THIS WEEKEND
Financial	• IN DEBT • BARELY PAYING THE BILLS • BILL COLLECTION AGENCIES CALLING MY HOUSE	• FINANCIALLY SECURE • A LARGE SAVINGS ACCOUNT	• FIND A BETTER PAYING JOB • STOP WASTING MONEY ON DRUGS • PAY ALL OLD BILLS	NOW
Legal	• THREE OUTSTANDING PARKING TICKETS • SPEEDING TICKET • INVOLVED IN A LAWSUIT — BEING SUED.	• FREE & CLEAR • NO WORRIES ABOUT LEGAL MATTERS	• GO SEE AN ATTORNEY	MONDAY MORNING
Education	• UNDER-TRAINED FOR JOB ADVANCEMENT • DROPPED OUT OF HIGH SCHOOL IN 11th GRADE	• HAVE A COLLEGE DEGREE	• FINISH HIGH SCHOOL & GET DIPLOMA • START NIGHT SCHOOL	AS SOON AS POSSIBLE

47

GET A LIFE !

Subject/Habit	Where are you now?	Where would you like to be?	What steps do you need to take?	When?
Health, Dietary	• Overweight • Loud/Constant Coughing • Limping	• Healthy in all areas	• Go see a doctor • Eat right	As soon as possible
Physical Exercise	• Overweight & tired all the time • Out of breath	• Strong & active • Muscular & in great shape	• Exercise regularly • Jog every other day • Take aerobics class • Lift weights at home	Now
Leisure Activities, Hobbies	• Few activities • Watch T.V. all the time - couch potato • No hobbies • Sleep a lot	• Enjoying fun activities • Spending time with my new creative & exciting hobby	• Exercise more • Stay off the couch & out of bed • Go outside & do something fun • Go to a hobby shop	This week
Self-Help/ Support Groups	• Alone all the time	• A part of several groups • Having people call me on the telephone	• Attend a support group meeting - regularly • Go to several different groups • Participate at the meetings • Go out for coffee after the meeting w/ someone from group	A.S.A.P.

48

GET A LIFE !

Changing one unhealthy habit requires changing many lifestyle habits. To gain control of one part of your life requires you to develop a balanced overall life. This guide will help you identify areas of your life you need to change, identify the destination you want to achieve, develop steps to reach that destination, and push you to take control as soon as possible.

Subject/Habit	Where are you now?	Where would you like to be?	What steps do you need to take?	When?
Family				
Intimate Relationships				
Employment/ Career				
Friendships				

GET A LIFE !

Subject/Habit	Where are you now?	Where would you like to be?	What steps do you need to take?	When?
Social Life, Group Organizations				
Financial				
Legal				
Education				

GET A LIFE !

Subject/Habit	Where are you now?	Where would you like to be?	What steps do you need to take?	When?
Health, Dietary				
Physical Exercise				
Leisure Activities, Hobbies				
Self-Help/ Support Groups				

people do." Others say, "My problem is with street drugs, not booze, so why does everyone tell me that I have to stop drinking?"

It's natural to want to strive for the moderation of our habits rather than total abstinence. I can't imagine anyone indulging in their unhealthy habit of choice and not deriving some compelling benefits. But the fact is, abstinence is substantially easier to achieve. If you doubt that, just think about all the times you were able to go on a very strict and rigid diet, or stop smoking, or abstain from alcohol, gambling or drugs -- only to find that once you started drinking occasionally, or cheating on your diet, or borrowing cigarettes, you soon ended up right back where you started. It has become a cliche, but it's still more than a good joke: "I can quit any time I want. I've done it thousands of times!"

Of course, the issue of moderation is not subject to discussion when your habits involve eating, spending, or relationships. With activities like these, moderation is the only option.

What kind of goals should you set if your habit doesn't involve food or life sustaining activities? Such behaviors include, but are not limited to: gambling, workaholism, over spending, hyper-sexuality, obsessions with pornography, excessive exercising, hypochondria and destructive relationships. These behavioral unhealthy habits need to be understood in the same way as addictions to psycho-active substances. While they appear to be judged by society much less harshly, they involve the same processes and you will need to use the same techniques to restore balance to your life.

You can begin by making a list of who you are, items that describe you in every detail. Now, make another list leaving out all your bad habits and see what potential for wonderful accomplishments you possess. You will notice that YOU are NOT your bad habit!

Develop your new life with activities that leave out, as much as possible, the stimulus that makes you want to indulge in your unhealthy habits. If you are in situations that motivate you to indulge in your unhealthy habit, and you want to try to moderate the habit, be sure that you are with a group of people who will support you and motivate you to stay within your pre-set limit of moderation. It is usually not wise to try to moderate your habit when you are alone. You will find it much more difficult to draw the line and stop by yourself.

I would also like to remind anyone who is considering moderate alcohol use of a few additional points. First, and most importantly, it is generally agreed by most experts today that moderation consists of two drinks per day for men and one drink a day for women. If you find yourself saying, "That's no fun!" "I can't even get high on one or two drinks," then perhaps moderation really isn't for you. Anything over these amounts is considered to be unhealthful by the medical community. Even these levels may be too much for some individuals. But if keeping alcohol in your life is still your goal, try it. If it works and you can keep your intake truly moderate, then continue. On the other hand, if you continue to fall back into your old habits, give yourself a break, take control and stop it completely.

If it is disturbing to you to think about not having another drink for the rest of your life, it might be helpful to abstain for three to six months before attempting moderation. This strategy serves several purposes. One, it can reduce your alcohol tolerance so that when you do resume drinking, a smaller amount will give you the desired effect. Secondly, during the months of abstinence, you will build self-confidence and learn new ways of coping with stress, anxiety, loneliness, and boredom. Thirdly, you may find that after a few months of abstinence, you feel so healthy and so good about yourself, that you will decide not to risk your new sense of well being by indulging at all. At the very least, with several months of sobriety under your belt, you can't help noticing by stark contrast any impairment caused by your resumed drinking. Remember, this is your life, and you have the power to make it better or worse.

Whatever habit it is you wish to change, you need to take sole responsibility. Give yourself all the chances you need to succeed. Just the stress of coping with an unhealthy habit wears the body and the mind down day-by-day. So, engage yourself, don't indulge yourself.

Remember, "Don't Kill Yourself, Skill Yourself!"

CHAPTER 1 OVERCOMING YOUR OBJECTIONS

PART 4 YOU ARE IN CONTROL

"To fall into a habit is to begin to cease to be." This quote by Miguel de Unamuno, a noted Spanish philosopher, poet, and novelist clearly reflects the strong control that unhealthy habits have over our lives. But, how does an unhealthy habit gain such powerful control over us?

It is quite simply a paradox (a statement or situation that is seemingly self-contradictory). More often than not, you begin an unhealthy habit so that you feel that you will have more control over your life. You feel that life is a mine field which is booby-trapped with hidden explosives that will blow your mental stability apart if you step on one. To you, life is full of terrors of the unknown just waiting to trap you, embarrass you, and strip you of your dignity; thereby, exposing to everyone what a fraud you really are. At first, by using your new protective bad habit it appears that you have gained substantially more control. If you are drinking, real life seems blurred, far away, and non-threatening. -- If you are compulsively shopping, you feel the exhilaration of spending money and acquiring new 'things' that are supposed to make you happier, more privileged, and more comfortable. -- If you are gambling, you feel the rush of the risk each time you bet, and you feel the power and importance that the casino situation seems to give you. -- If you are an hypochondriac, you reap the benefits of sympathy and special attention showered on you from others, while their expectations of your performance are lessened because your illness has reduced your capability to perform 100%. -- And, if you are smoking cigarettes, you feel that you have something to do with your hands that covers the weakness of your shyness, and you feel that you look more sophisticated or even perhaps older and wiser. Of course, these are but a few examples of crippling, unhealthy habits.

All these "controls" that you are seeking with your bad habit do seem to work for a while, but as time passes, they narrow your life. They project you into their own little world and make you a slave who serves them. Some habits become so severe and all consuming that people find that they have to create very private and secret lives for themselves, just so they can serve their habit without the glaring and disapproving eyes of the public.

The paradox is that the same power of mind and mental control that you used to create and serve these unhealthy habits is the same strength of mind that you still possess to decide to change your life and develop a new and more rewarding lifestyle.

Can people really learn to stop on their own? Contrary to the statements of many 12 step programs and self-improvement courses and clinics, current national surveys have shown that large percentages of people are in fact successful at quitting a wide variety of unhealthy habits all by themselves. Those who are successful are almost twice as likely to succeed as those who use formal programs! Many new studies are now documenting that problem drinkers, street drug addicts, cigarette smokers, overeaters, gamblers, compulsive shoppers, and hypochondriacs can and do stop their unhealthy behaviors without formal professional intervention. This proves that "natural recovery" is fact rather than myth. So, the control that you seek over your life has always been there, it has just been used in a misdirected way. Yes, you are in control, you always were in control, and you always will be in control!

This lifetime training manual offers you the keys for taking control of making effective life changes, at your own pace, and in privacy, if you desire. Within this framework, those who suffer from all kinds of destructive, repetitive, unhealthy behaviors can design and start their own personal program of change while gaining more control of their lives.

This is not to suggest that this book promotes isolation on your part, but rather it helps you accept responsibility for changing yourself. This book encourages you to reach out, within a model that makes intuitive common sense, to whatever external resources are best suited to you as an individual. Whether you utilize support groups, church attendance, individual or family therapy, or a combination of these, you have brought these resources into your life and you have decided which tools to use. It is only when you are forced to utilize a particular tool, or are told to achieve a particular goal that you don't really desire, that we have treatment failures.

Difficulties with alcohol, overeating, street drug abuse, misuse of prescription medication, compulsive gambling, compulsive shopping, compulsive sexual behavior, etc. continue to plague vast numbers of our population. Those who are not directly troubled are frequently victimized by members of the family, co-workers, friends, etc. that do have unhealthy habits. These are the innocent victims of those practicing unhealthy lifestyle management habits. So, in a true sense, this book addresses all of us. In offering new alternatives, it offers what we all seek -- genuine well-founded hope.

One final word at the closing of this chapter -- about focusing on one unhealthy habit at a time. It is important to isolate one primary unhealthy habit and focus only on it. However, no unhealthy habit is independent. Strong or primary unhealthy habits always have minor or less obvious unhealthy habits orbiting around them. If you work on defeating the primary habit exclusively, the minor habits will usually cause the primary habit to return. In changing one habit permanently, many habits must be changed simultaneously or consecutively.

I feel that I must tell you that I have had certain clients whose primary unhealthy habit was such a dominating part of their life that I had them start working on defeating secondary or minor habits first. Once they gained those skills, they could tackle their primary habit with the confidence of knowing they could succeed. However, as a rule, my example of attacking only one major habit at a time works well for most people. After the first habit is under control, move on to the next habit, and so forth.

As you develop a new healthy lifestyle, make it a point to create it around activities that you truly in your heart of hearts, enjoy. For example, do not take up bowling as a diversion to drinking, only to fall back on drinking at some later date because you always found bowling to be dull and boring. In the end, it will fail to take the place of alcohol.

Don't lie to yourself about anything. Don't fool yourself into believing something will work for you just because it looks easy on the surface, or that it has worked well for someone else. This is your chance to do something wonderful with your own life. This is honestly your chance to restructure your life into something that will really please you and support you.

Remember, it is your duty to "Skill Yourself and Not Kill Yourself!"

Now, that we have faced and overcome your objections, let's proceed with renewed spirit, conviction and resolve, knowing that we are in control -- and are headed for a new more fulfilling life of healthy habits.

TAKE CONTROL NOW!

CHAPTER 2 FACING THE DRAGON

PART 1 AM I THE DRAGON?

"Alone, alone, all, all alone;

Alone on a wide, wide sea."

This quote from Samuel Taylor's poem "The Rhyme of the Ancient Mariner" perhaps best sums up how you feel as you begin to leave your unhealthy habits behind. You will find yourself saying things like: "It's just not worth it." - "I'm in too far over my head to quit." - "This is too scary." - "This is just too big for me to handle." - "I feel that I'm losing control." - "I feel like a ship adrift with no engine and no rudder."

Historically, all unhealthy habits have been seen as a sign of some moral failing or lack of willpower. Today, professionals around the world see all types of habits as just part of the human condition. The most important thing to remember is that if you are now in the process of replacing your unhealthy behavior with healthy habits you should place no shame and no blame on yourself or anyone or anything in your life. Trying to shift the focus onto a disease, a weakness, your upbringing or another person will only slow your progress down. Even if you discover the origin of your habit, nothing will change. A habit gains a life of its own well before it takes on the overt characteristics of the behavior that you recognize as a habit. You are where you are now. Deal with your present situation -- where you find yourself now. It is counterproductive and wastes much of your time trying to assign shame or blame for your unhealthy habits. Understand that you do have unhealthy habits that you are trying to replace with healthy habits and work on doing that only. Focus on your future and look at yourself as being a braided rope. As you leave your unhealthy habits behind the

Am I my own dragon?

braided rope begins to unravel. You like the rope, will still have kinks, but over time the kinks will slowly come out. But rebraid the rope by going back to your former unhealthy habits and the kinks will come back quickly; and the process will need to begin again.

Remember what you have learned about yourself in Chapter One. Remember the exercises that you have done about ambivalence and making excuses. Remember that you are now developing a strong Internal Locus (Point) of Control that will enable you to accomplish more than you ever dreamed. Only by taking control will you not lose more control as you gain new more powerful control of your life in developing healthy habits.

As we examine the things we become addicted to, whether it is gambling, shopping, work and stress, food, drugs, alcohol, or hypersexuality, there is always an arousal component. Another fundamental element of all unhealthy habits is that they change our mood, energy or arousal level. If a substance or behavior does not accomplish this, then it will not be sought after, and repeated again and again. No one, for example, becomes addicted to celery. Did you ever wonder why there is no 'Celery Eaters Anonymous?' This may sound like a foolish question, but it is central to understanding why only particular substances and behaviors seem to compel us, and why only certain people become addicted to these things while others only enjoy them in moderation as a normal part of their lives. It is important to know the answer to these questions in your learning how to free yourself from the destructive relationship you have with any or all of these behaviors.

We human beings are all creatures of habit, and habits are nothing more than repetitive behavior. Without habits, we simply couldn't function. All of us engage in repetitive behavior patterns thousands of times every day as we go about our familiar routines performing basic tasks by rote. Without these habit patterns we would have to

Why don't people become addicted to celery?

reinvent ourselves and our lives on a daily basis. This may sound shocking, but just try to imagine what it would be like to perform every action -- from brushing your teeth in the morning, to turning off the lights at night -- as though you were doing these things for the first time! The amount of energy and concentration required from you would be enormous. Such a life would be intolerable, stressful, and chaotic. It would leave you unequipped to function on any kind of productive level.

Unhealthy lifestyle management habits are simply one end of this repetitive continuum. It is the negative end of a whole host of repetitive methods of coping with life and attaining rewards. Unhealthy habits have many negative consequences that cause our lives to go awry, but we feel unable to discontinue our behavior in spite of these negative repercussions.

As we discussed earlier, the difference between negative habits and positive habits are as follows: Negative habits are those which initially produce good feelings, followed by pain and discomfort. Drinking feels good at first, but is followed by a hang-over. Positive habits, on the other hand, have the discomfort up front followed by delayed gratification, like the pain of exercise followed by a rewarding gain in physical health. A habit can be like a coin, one side makes you feel better, the other side makes you feel worse. The question is, with which side of the coin do you wish to start.

There is no such thing as an unhealthy habit that is either entirely biological or psychological. As we have discussed in Chapter One, there are sociological, biological, and psychological components involved in all behavior. After being exposed to a substance or a behavior on a sociological level through friends, advertising, or by accident, which comes first in the development of an unhealthy habit -- the biological or the psychological? It boils down to the old question, "Which came first, the chicken or the egg?" I have personally found that both factors are in play, at different strengths, at different times, and that each affects the other.

For example, I once treated a high school girl who started drinking in response to peer pressure. She was introduced to beer on a sociological level by her friends, and then the friends put pressure on her to be "one of the group" by drinking until she was drunk. The peer pressure is a psychological component. After she drank alcohol, it set up biological mechanisms which changed her mood. Linda told me, "After two or three drinks, I started to feel pretty high and I forgot about the strange new taste of it. There was this good looking boy on the football team, I really liked him a lot, and after I got a little tipsy, we started joking around and I just felt really good." The result was that this change in mood contributed to her even greater psychological drive to drink again. It is generally a back-and-forth, see-saw sort of process. To make this an either-or dispute is not productive, and only imposes limitations which can seriously inhibit change and growth.

This brings us to the question, "Is there an addictive personality?" According to research literature, the "Addictive Personality" has been something scientists have been totally unable to define and classify. As a clinician however, I continue to be amazed at some clients who seem to go from one addiction to the next -- from giving up one habit to developing a new one just as quickly. Similarly, these clients seem to get addicted to virtually everything they come into contact with that is unhealthy for them. They come in to see me for an alcohol problem, but they also smoke cigarettes, gamble too much, and/or become workaholics who are addicted to stress and pressure.

My belief is that there are several personality styles or types (or combinations of them) that relate to or interact with substances and behavioral activities in such a way that causes them to become addicted easily. One type of addictive personality is rooted mainly in Biological Processes. A second type is the "Short-Cut Seeker." Way back in a person's childhood, there were some forks in the road. The forks were between leaning on Mom, food, money, or other things outside of themselves to feel good versus realizing that leaning on outside things puts them in a dependent position and therefore not in their best interest. Another way of saying this is that some people see that leaning on these "Elixirs" keep them dependent while others look at "Elixirs" as keeping them in control. It is interesting to note that those who see Elixirs as giving them control tend to seek more Elixirs for even greater control. These people also find themselves addicted to many different types of behaviors and substances. Leaning on Elixirs from childhood sets the stage for never developing proper internal controls, and therefore leads to them remaining dependent on someone or something. This is exactly why celery is not addictive, it doesn't change our mood.

Let's continue our discussion on arousal. It is essentially a phenomenon of the central nervous system. Most of us fluctuate between very low levels of arousal in the morning, to the highest level around lunchtime, to a low level again before falling asleep. We are somewhere in between the extremes virtually all day long. Our optimal level at noon is going to be different from our optimal level at bedtime. When you are in "sync" with your typical schedule for a particular time of day, you feel comfortable with and about yourself. You are at your optimum level, even though your optimal points will vary throughout a 24-hour day.

Arousal varies from a high point of abject terror to the lowest point which is a state of coma. However, the middle range of arousal is where most of us feel the greatest degree of comfort. That level for many people is experienced around noon each day, when they are feeling good about themselves -- producing well, not hungover from the night before and not under too much stress.

At very low levels of arousal, both feelings and performance respond accordingly. When we are tired or bored, we lack the energy to perform at our peak. Similarly, at high levels of arousal, our feelings are a disturbance. We are usually uptight and uncomfortable; we find that we are unable to concentrate which in turn impedes our performance. Therefore, it is only at moderate levels of arousal that our feelings enable us to function at our best.

Research suggests that each of us has what is called a Diurnal [arousal] Cycle. We normally wake-up, experience various levels of energy and fall asleep at approximately the same time every day and night. Most of us are born with a relatively low amplitude Diurnal Cycle. We peak at adolescence and then start to decline, with less and less overall energy as we grow older. Basically, our arousal patterns remain constant throughout our lives, although there are some people who are born with or acquire a more "laid-back" or passive/restful nature. Hyperactive people, on the other hand, have an overall high amplitude of arousal. Those whose levels peak at midnight are called "night people." It doesn't matter what the shape or amplitude of your arousal cycle is. You have become accustomed to it and that is what is important.

There is a wide variety of potentially unhealthy substances and activities whose use may originate in attempts to self-regulate the arousal levels. If you are below the desired level, you will probably reach for coffee or turn on some 'rock' music. If you are above your optimal level, you might drink a glass of wine or listen to soothing music. Without realizing it, we have become creatures of self-regulation, using these substances and activities as a means of regulating and controlling our moods.

It is interesting to note, that not only are there singular uses of substances or shortcuts, there are also multiple uses. For example, the performer, John Belushi, died from using a mixture of heroin and cocaine at the same time: one is a depressant, and the other is a stimulant. Here is an extreme example of someone using multiple substances to 'Fine-Tune' himself. One drug in isolation would perhaps cause the user to fall below the optimal level, while the other drug alone might elevate one's mood too high. In combination, however, the person practicing unhealthy behavior habits hopes to produce a desirable mood/performance state for a time.

This is obviously reckless and dangerous behavior, and reaches into the areas of maximum unhealthy behavior habits. As a person viewing it from the outside it is clear and obvious. However, for the person accustomed to practicing this sort of unhealthy behavior, it has become the "norm" and gives them the illusion of being in control. Therefore, it is more difficult for him/her to see the harmful results. At some point, your unhealthy behavior habits will become so dominant that you will recognize the negative effects on your life and health, and it is at that time you are in a position to make a conscious decision to save yourself and redevelop healthy lifestyle habits.

I believe that over time, we learn to become extremely fine-tuned chemists in regard to regulating our nervous systems, choosing and mixing multiple substances and activities to regulate our arousal levels. A common example is the association of alcohol with smoking. A great many people smoke cigarettes when they drink. Alcohol sedates and nicotine in the cigarette stimulates, so we use cigarettes to overcome the alcohol's sedative effect.

While a certain amount of self-regulatory behavior is both normal and necessary, there are basically two types of people who get into trouble with this mechanism. Extreme "Type-A" people [hyperactive, highly competitive] prefer a very high level of arousal, which means they are bound to fall below their optimal level at some point during the day. This causes them to constantly seek out activities that will raise their level of arousal such as noisy parties, motorcycles, fast cars, loud music, etc.

"Type-B" people, on the other hand, tend to be "laid-back" and "low-key." These individuals like to feel calm and prefer very low levels of arousal. When they feel tense, as invariably happens in today's high-stress world of freeways, job pressure, and social stress, they typically search out ways of calming down to reach their optimum level. They favor hot tubs, soft music, a relaxing book, or a tranquilizer.

It is important to realize which basic "Type" you are and to understand that at extreme levels you are probably "missing the mark," either trying to over-sedate or over-stimulate yourself. While you may have started in life close to middle ground, both genetic and environmental factors can alter your arousal needs. This is especially true when you learn to manipulate these levels through artificial short-cuts which push you further toward the extreme.

When this happens, you need to learn to do two things. First, if you're a high-level person, you must bring your level back down. If you prefer low levels, you need to learn how to tolerate higher degrees of arousal. Secondly, both Types must master alternative strategies that do not require either unhealthy substances or behaviors.

CHARTING YOUR DAILY AROUSAL/ENERGY LEVEL

Date ___MAY 3___

Day of the week ___TUESDAY___

Week ___#2___

Your Arousal/Energy Level

Time of Day

69

CHARTING YOUR DAILY AROUSAL/ENERGY LEVEL

Date _____
Day of the week_____
Week _____

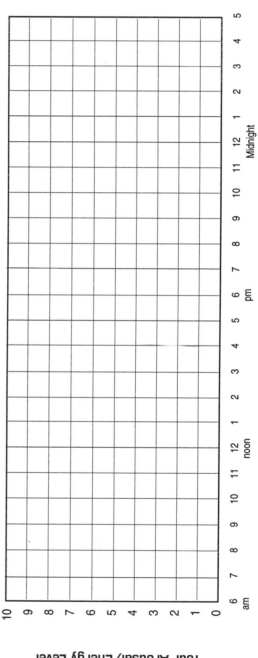

Your Arousal/Energy Level

10
9
8
7
6
5
4
3
2
1
0

6 am 7 8 9 10 11 12 noon 1 2 3 4 5 6 pm 7 8 9 10 11 12 Midnight 1 2 3 4 5

Time of Day

70

CHAPTER 2 FACING THE DRAGON

PART 2 HOW DID THE DRAGON CATCH ME?

I have tried to find a way to explain the narrowing of coping responses, accompanied by an increasing preoccupation with the bad habit of choice, and I thought of this example which I call "The Five Finger Exercise."

Take your hand and place it on the table. Now, stretch out all five fingers and balance your hand on your fingertips. Feel how stable your hand is when all your fingers are in play. But what happens if you move one or more fingers away? You have the very strong feeling that your stability and balance are slipping away, but you are still able to maintain a balance.

This is exactly what the process of adaptation to your habit is all about. At one time in our lives, most of us were balanced on all "five fingers." Our world was filled with clubs, organizations, music, sports, hobbies, and relationships. What happened to disturb that stability is that we became bored, insecure, or unhappy. We found that we were in need of stimulation to over-ride the problem, and we could no longer rely on the gratification of clubs, music, sports, etc. to do that. So, we looked for a "short-cut life" answer, and we found things like food, shopping, alcohol, street drugs, working long stressful hours, gambling, etc. that gave us the instant, but temporary, feeling that everything was good and that we had no real problems. Being creatures who innately understand emotional gratification and the rewards of emotional control, we began to gradually put less and less energy into the old activities that "left us wanting," and ultimately our balance started to shift from five fingers to four, then to three, on to two and finally just one -- which became our

71

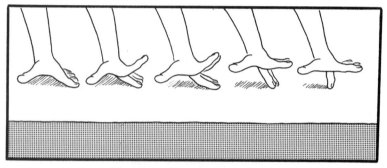

The Five Finger Exercise

satisfying unhealthy habit of choice. When we are balanced only on one finger, we are 100% committed to that one unhealthy habit. We are left with only one temporary way to make ourselves feel better. We find that to feel better, we need more and/or larger doses of the unhealthy habit -- we are trapped in a prison of our own device. What can we do?

One size does not fit all! There is not one answer for everyone. While some people practicing unhealthy lifestyle habits require professional assistance, many others can learn to either stop their behavior totally or achieve healthy moderation, as we have already discussed. You will find your own solution partially by not lying to yourself, by being committed to a healthful change, and by developing a strong Internal Locus (Point) of Control.

UNLEARNING -- HOW COPING SKILLS WERE UNLEARNED

The greatest seduction that unhealthy habits possess is that they appear to work, and work effectively, for a wide variety of uncomfortable emotions and behaviors. The problem is that every time you take the path of the "short-cut" solution, you "unlearn" a more adaptive way of coping. Each time you take the longer "coping skill" method, you learn a new skill. So, over time, if you take the short-cut method, you begin to unlearn more and more life-skills. Many clients of mine knew how to be sociable before they found beer, or how to fall asleep before they found sleeping medications. The longer you have been taking the short-cut method, the more you unlearn, and the less new information you learn. Many people, over time, unlearn basic skills and replace them with unhealthy habits that act as walls that prevent them from accepting new information and learning new skills. These walls act as a barrier between you and your natural coping skills and rob you of the independence and freedom in life that was your natural birthright.

GETTING OUT OF YOUR COMFORT ZONE

One of the primary steps in taking control of healthy lifestyle habits is to get out of your comfort zone. In all of our lives we settle into a lifestyle where we are not threatened or pressured -- this is our comfort zone. We don't have to learn any more to get by, we don't have to buy anything more to get by, we don't have to do anything outside our area of responsibility just to get by. No one will threaten us, no one will motivate us, no one will challenge us, in other words -- we are comfortable.

You must burst out of your comfort zone. You must "Face Your Dragon" that is your unhealthy habit. You must look it in the eye, know it for what it is and what it is doing to you, and you must have a vision or a plan to rid yourself of it in order to develop a rewarding and healthy lifestyle for yourself. You must take your self-imposed limited horizons and turn them into wide vistas of opportunity for you. This is not an easy thing to do; however, if you have the intention, the commitment, the integrity, and the responsibility, you will find it much easier. These are the four steps to breaking through the walls of the comfort zone. Let's take a closer look at them:

- Intention = Is what you want. A strong desire, a determination to make the change to a healthy lifestyle.

- Commitment = Is the energy that you devote to every moment that supports your intention to live a healthy lifestyle.

- Integrity = Is what is true for you right now. Telling the truth to yourself, about yourself and making that truth a tool for improvement.

74

- Responsibility = Is the ability to respond. It breaks the old unhealthy stimulus/response pattern and allows you to have great influence on the choices you make in life each day.

If any one of these practices are not in your life, they will ALL be imbalanced, just like the "Five Finger Exercise." When you are in balance, you are achieving your goal of leaving the comfort zone with a perfect mixture of intention, commitment, integrity, and with the ability to respond to the moment with awareness and satisfaction of accomplishment. These are all ways of putting fingers back down to give you support and structure.

When you leave the "black zone" (non-productive, stagnant life) of your comfort zone, you will suddenly find that you are motivated again by thoughts and things that were always important to you but have been asleep within you. Such personal motivators are:

- Feeling that my real skills and capabilities have the potential of being put to use for my own betterment.
- Being fair with myself.
- Having less and less self-doubt each day.
- Feeling that I am an important individual.
- Being able to explore healthy new areas, and grow as much as I can.
- Using my own initiative to accomplish a goal.
- Knowing what is going on in my life, not lying to myself.
- Knowing what I expect of myself.
- Recognizing my own accomplishments, and enjoying new feelings of self-worth.

- Tolerating my own mistakes without self-depreciation.

- Knowing that my standards for myself are high and I can reach them.

- Attaining and feeling the real rewards of meeting my own standards.

In taking control of your live, it is important to know and understand your internal/personal motivators and to set absolute standards for your life that embody your beliefs, integrity, and ethics. You must use these motivators and absolute standards in the on-going practice of "Skilling Yourself, Not Killing Yourself."

How do we set standards for ourselves?

- Standards should be set by you and you alone -- don't accept other people's standards as your own.

- Set fair and attainable standards for yourself.

- Write down what you expect. Intangible results should be written down in simple and clear language.

- Standards must be consistent and compatible with each other. Confusion or counterproductive standards will hinder your progress.

- Theoretical ideas should be avoided. Keep standards in the real world. Remember: "Skill Yourself, Don't Kill Yourself!"

CHAPTER 2 FACING THE DRAGON

PART 3 CHANGING CHANNELS

"YOU HOLD THE REMOTE CONTROL TO YOUR LIFE!"

Another important function of having unhealthy substances and behaviors in your life

is to assist you in 'changing channels.' To understand this concept, imagine that you are

watching Channel Two on television, which is featuring a horror movie that is extremely

scary and unsettling to you. If you don't like watching blood and gore, you simply take the

remote control and -- click, it's gone -- you are watching a game show on Channel Four.

Remember, the show that disturbed you on Channel Two is still running, but you are no

longer thinking about that; instead, you are focused on the questions being asked on the game

show. You have successfully changed your consciousness by directing your attention away

from something you don't want to think about to something that is more pleasant for you.

The ease with which we have learned to change television channels is directly related

to the way in which you use your unhealthy habits. Drinking, overeating, compulsive

shopping, overworking in a stressful atmosphere and gambling, all enable you to quickly

change emotional/thinking and thought direction; in essence, you have changed 'thought'

channels.

Thrill seeking does the same thing. Did you ever get behind the wheel of your car

and drive so fast that you literally "put your problems behind you?" At 80 mph and above,

you have no choice but to focus all your attention on the road. All potentially unhealthy

Unhealthy habits are not solving your problem –
It's just "changing the channel."

behaviors share the same feature -- the ability to change channels, quickly and with very little effort.

In fact, much of our society today has been seduced into a lifestyle that encourages and promotes changing channels. That is one of the reasons that so many people spend hours in front of the television, immediately turn on the radio when they enter their car, or become movie addicts. This need for fantasy and escape has become pervasive, and in some cases, destructive. Under the guise of relaxation and thanks to modern technology, we have been seduced "to get away from" our feelings, moods, and thoughts. If it's uncomfortable, don't think about it -- don't feel anything! Turn on your "Walkman," "Watchman," or "Game Boy" -- Sit in front of your computer, watch a video movie, turn up the stereo, watch the sports channel for hours on end, go to a party, or play a video game by yourself or with others. Let's not talk about any of our problems -- ever! Our 'escapist society' allows us to run in many tempting directions escaping our problems and the real world.

As we bury our problems under a mountain of technological diversions, we also bury pieces of ourselves. Soon, we become a "fugitive from life itself." Soon, there is so little of our 'real selves' left unburied that we have become programmed androids going about the day's activities only a ghost of our former selves. And it goes on, and on, and on. Finally, we find that we have lost our healthy coping responses to life's situations and we don't develop new ones because an unhealthy habit works efficiently and effectively every time.

To better understand the entrapping nature of unhealthy habits, let's try to identify and understand the motives which led you there.

All of us like (and want) to feel in control. Life is unpredictable at best. We can't always know what lies around the bend ahead. We might meet an old friend or it could be a

'Jack-the-Ripper' type of character. This world that we live in is often frightening and is always stressful. We Americans live in what is quite possibly the most complex society ever to exist. Not only are our personal roles multi-faceted, but we are constantly called upon to make decisions based on limited knowledge. When I went into a supermarket as a child, there were 10 to 12 different brands of breakfast cereal from which to choose. Now, there may be 50 to 60, all competing for my attention. Although this is a rather simple example it is representative of the countless stress-producing decisions we encounter every day. Of course, that is in addition to major life decisions involving our career, finances, family and marriage.

Granted we human beings have created our own "Stress Monster" by making everything so complicated and difficult to learn or understand. The stress and complexity of our civilization often makes us feel "Out of Control." When we feel that way, we are understandably uncomfortable. Therefore, we might want to compensate by seeking activities and behaviors which provide at least the "Illusion of Control." The pathway that we follow most frequently to gain that "Illusion of Control" is "Short-Cut Life." These shortcuts serve the function of giving us the sense of "Being in Charge," of being able to master our feelings our moods and our arousal levels. This mastery is an illusion because we have grasped onto something outside of ourselves (outside of our mind's natural coping skills) that sets the stage for dependence on unhealthy habits.

Let me offer an example of this. A speaker is scheduled to give a speech in front of a large, important audience. He is understandably nervous, which shoots his anxiety level up well beyond his comfort zone. Fearful that his performance will be terrible due to his nervousness and fear, he takes a Valium (a tranquilizer). Once the pill takes affect, he feels more relaxed and confident; and as a result, he delivers his speech quite well. He walks away not only feeling pleased, but inwardly believing that he could not perform as well again without the aid of the Valium. Thus, what appeared to provide a sense of mastery over his mood, eventually will develop into something which will have control over him. The steps of the process are as follows:

- Step 1   =   Anxiety or discomfort.

- Step 2   =   A shortcut solution is found.

- Step 3   =   A successful result is perceived.

- Step 4   =   Pride in accomplishment is felt along with increased expectations by self and others to maintain this high level of performance.

- Step 5   =   A belief grows that the shortcut is an essential ingredient of success.

- Step 6   =   Reduced self-confidence results because of the false perception that the task cannot be performed well without using the shortcut.

- Step 7   =   Greater reliance on the shortcut is developed along with a deepening relationship with quick-fix solutions.

As you can clearly see, what appeared as a means of control turns into conditioned helplessness and hopelessness in the face of emotional discomfort and life's daily challenges.

You will find that the 'control factor' also has relevance and meaning when it comes to denial. When you are confronted by someone who tells you that they think you are dependent on an unhealthy habit, you might say: "I enjoy it, but I'm not dependent." What you are really saying is that you have the illusion of control. You view your substance or

81

behavior of choice as something you can manage or handle, but actually it is the substance or behavior that is controlling you!

Tranquilizers such as Valium or Xanax are prime examples of this. After several months of using these mood altering drugs, your arousal level does become lower and you find that stress affects you less and less. You may like this lower lever of arousal so much that you start to carry the pills around with you. You know they work quickly and effectively, and they have become your "emotional security blanket" that helps protect you from the daily stresses and challenges of life.

Last year, I was working with a talented young actress who used the tranquilizer Xanax. In her words, "They keep me in control when I'm on the set." After taking the drug every day during a long and demanding film shoot, she began carrying the pills in her purse, whether she was working or not. "I just wanted to have them with me, in case I get called for a reading or an audition. It just makes me feel better knowing they're there."

At this point, her denial became a matter of rationalizing her statements. "I wasn't hooked or anything like that," she went on, "It was just nice knowing that I had the power to control a situation when I wanted to."

That is exactly where the seductiveness of the substance or activity comes into play. They quietly sneak into your life, giving you the illusion of mastery over your mood, your emotions, your levels of activity, even your destiny -- and they dominate you. It is a form of "Changing Channels" and a destructive delusion of your own competence, which in the end, leaves you with no real skills in coping with life.

The English poet George Grabbe wrote the following pertinent lines:

"Habit with him was all the test of truth,

It must be right, I've done it from my youth."

Remember, the unhealthy habit has been with you so long that you have become used to it. It has become a hidden but very powerful and controlling force in your life. Start now to be very aware of it, and it's control over you. Stop lying to yourself about who is in control. Start to replace your unhealthy habit little by little, and it will become weaker and weaker, until your new healthy lifestyle can replace it with a more satisfying and rewarding life for you.

Always keep in mind that in making a lifestyle change: "Don't Kill Yourself, Skill Yourself!"

TAKE CONTROL NOW!

CHAPTER 2   FACING THE DRAGON

PART 4   SHORT-CUT SOLUTIONS

"The woods are lovely, dark and deep,

But I have promises to keep,

And miles to go before I sleep --

And miles to go before I sleep."

This quote from Robert Frost's poem 'Stopping by Woods on a Snowy Evening'
reflects beautifully on how you must be feeling at this point of the book. The woods being
lovely, dark, and deep reflects the safety and familiarity of your bad habit, but you know
that you are on the road to developing healthy habits -- after all, you have made your most
excellent promise to yourself that you will. Although you are firmly committed, and have
made a good start on developing healthy habits, it will take some time to do it, so you 'have
miles to go before you sleep' and finally reach your desired goal.

Let's return for a moment to the example of the speaker who used the tranquilizer
Valium just before making a difficult speech. He also illustrates what I call "The Circle of
Addiction." The Valium-taker, if he performs well, walks away with an outer sense of pride
of accomplishment, control and the inner belief that the Valium pill will ensure his success
the next time as well.

As you may remember from the example, it started with him being nervous about his
speech. Then he took a Valium pill and he performed well. So, the foundation of emotional
self-control is built on having the drug. His inner self-confidence, therefore, goes down
because, he now believes that he cannot handle anxiety without chemical help from the pill.

84

The next time he walks onto stage, he will be even more nervous and non-confident, and therefore, he has a greater need for the quick-fix of the pill. This man, in essence, was seduced into an adaptive cycle without realizing it. He is now more apt than ever to return to the addictive behavior. I am convinced that within severely addicted individuals who practice unhealthy habits, there are hundreds of these circles taking place on many levels.

With an unhealthy habit circular addiction, you are giving yourself the illusion that you are controlling the problem, but it is a false control. Each time you solve your problem with your unhealthy habit, you are fooling yourself with a short-term solution that can never, and will never, have any permanent effect at all. It is a quick and dirty fix leading you nowhere, just in a circle, like a dog chasing his tail. You have taught yourself to be helpless -- and you have lost your natural coping skills.

Another example of biological circular unhealthy habits is the 'hangover.' Let's say that you're feeling hungover from drinking the night before. So, you have another drink to "get you going" the next morning. Starting early, you are likely to have a lot more drinks before the day is over.

As day follows night, when you wake up the next morning, you will have another hangover. Of course, the best way to recover is to repeat the process. It is like a snake that bites it's own tail, it forms a perfect circle.

Another important example is the vicious cycle of someone caught in an extremely stress producing job position. The job stress situation might look like this:

- Severe job pressure and stress.

- To cope with the stress, they turn to unhealthy habits centering around: food, liquor, prescription medication, street drugs, gambling, hypersexuality, or compulsive shopping.

- The unhealthy habit(s) cause them not to be able to think clearly or perform their duties as well as is expected. They cannot even plan clearly how to find another job which would have less pressure and stress.

- They remain trapped in the same old job, under the same stressful situations.

- The stress and pressure continues to build, and so do their circular cycles of bad habits.

The psychological circle of unhealthy habits is illustrated by the man who can't ask a woman to dance at a party unless he has had a few cocktails. He is so nervous that he downs a couple of drinks which numbs his shyness and then approaches her. When she accepts, and he has a wonderful time with her the rest of the evening, he is convinced that he cannot make a move without first fortifying himself with liquor.

I often tell my clients whose unhealthy habit is drinking too much that alcohol has no properties which enhance their coordination, dancing abilities, or potential of acceptance when asking another person to dance.

What happens to everyone practicing unhealthy habits is that they now attribute certain abilities to the power of a particular substance or behavior. These shortcuts become addictions when biological, psychological, and sociological adaptations seduce us and become the controlling mechanisms. We are drawn into that circle of unhealthy habits once the effect of a substance or a behavior creates the need within us for more, and more, and more. The more successful the "short-cut life" tactic is in initially solving a problem, the greater the likelihood that it will attract us back into the circular cycle without ever giving us any sort of lasting solution, except that we need more and more of the bad habit to gain the effects that we had the first time that we tried it.

A very important and timely portrayal of circular unhealthy habits is the person who is a prisoner of job stress. We sometimes call them the "Workaholic." This person gets more emotional 'payoffs' at the office or job site than they do at home. So, they works harder and harder causing their family to feel more and more neglected and angry, which causes matters at home to worsen. They then feel even less positive about the home situation and feels compelled to stay at work even longer hours, because it is the only place where he/she can build self-esteem and feel important. This is also true for the un-married person who has no one at home. To this individual, home is a temporary place, like a hotel room that offers no comfort, so there is no need to hurry back there at the end of the day. Going home to an empty and hollow existence is equally as bad as going home to a hostile family situation. The result is that their world centers around the workplace. Stress becomes a substitute for happiness, with stress and over-work becoming the unhealthy habit. This person is like a mouse on a treadmill, hopelessly running in endless circles at top speed just going nowhere and getting there fast! This type of person constantly complains about pressure and stress, but has developed a need and craving for it.

This looks like a pretty grim picture -- but the circle can be broken. Since everything starts with needs and feelings, you must understand them, identify them and start to break the cycle consciously.

Courage is the control of fear, and it is somewhat frightening to start to de-program these unhealthy habits. But, just as when you were a child, once the fears were identified and "laid on the table" in the clear light of day, they lost a great deal of their impact. You must have the courage to face the fear, define it, dissect it, reduce it's negative impact, and replace it by developing healthy habits.

It takes bravery to look the dragon in the eye! Now that you own that bravery, it is time to take control! The birth and development of your Internal Locus (Point) of Control will enable you to stretch the envelope of your life. Nurture your own creativity, don't be a martyr. You must own your emotions, so that you can manage your mood swings and feelings about situations as they arise during the day. Do not fall back into the old familiar destructive habits.

Now is the time to take ownership of yourself and to see yourself as a whole. With your Internal Locus (Point) of Control, you have developed a healing presence in your mind. There is now a connectedness between your mind and body. You have developed a mind/body approach to developing healthy habits. You may have a time of grief over the loss of your unhealthy habits, but you are not helpless or hopeless any longer. You are now in a position where you are promoting and developing the good things about yourself. Your emotions play a big part in developing healthy habits and you are starting to own your emotions more and more each day. You are no longer a victim of emotional whims, rages, and rituals. You are indeed 'Facing your Dragons' and like knights of old -- conquering them!

TAKE CONTROL NOW!

CHAPTER 3 START TO TAKE CONTROL!

BREAKING THE CIRCLE

The merry-go-round glides smoothly around and around, its beautiful multi-colored lights and fancy carved horses are reflected in its big silver mirrors in a swirl of fanciful delight. The music plays and you can even try to grab the brass ring if you want, but no matter how long you stay on board, no matter how long you ride, you will still be in the same place. There is no "next destination" on a merry-go-round. It may be pretty to look at, but it takes you nowhere!

The only way to stop a merry-go-round ride is to make the conscious decision to get off and go somewhere else or do something else.

"I'll quit smoking as soon as I get the situation at work straightened out." - "I'll start going to the gym tomorrow." - "When Rick moves in I won't need to take tranquilizer pills anymore because I won't be alone at night." - "I'll start my diet after the holiday season."

Do these merry-go-round statements seem familiar? Such good intentions are recited millions of times every week as people just like you prepare to give up their destructive behaviors and habits, and move on to a better way of living. But these statements naively suggest that only limited behavior changes are necessary. They are changes involving either the reduction or elimination of a substance or behavior that has become an unhealthy habit.

Unfortunately however, letting go of an all engrossing unhealthy habit entails much more than merely cutting back on a particular indulgence. It means changing a whole series of emotionally-charged behaviors, thoughts, and activities. Only by shifting your entire laundry list of related habits can you achieve a stable change, and therefore successfully develop healthy habits.

This sounds like an overwhelming and difficult task. You can do it -- if you accept responsibility and start trying to understand the process (the Dragon) which has trapped you. Try to focus on what you will gain rather than focusing on what you are giving up.

We have discussed the circles of unhealthy habits. As you will remember, we discussed the Workaholic. That person's unhealthy habit not only involves the physical act of working, but all the attendant activities, thoughts and feelings about themself which contribute to the problem. But even beyond the overt actions of stress and work compulsions, this person may be locked in place by the attitudes and expectations of friends, co-workers, and family.

JANET'S STORY, "THE DIET"

Janet is an attractive, but overweight, high school teacher in her early forties. She worries about her large appearance and her concerns about being overweight leading to heart disease have prompted her to yet another attempt at dieting. She is watching her food intake and walking at least three miles a day, but nothing else has changed. Janet still hides a Hershey chocolate bar in her dresser, she jokes with her students, saying "Fat teachers are more easy-going," and even after losing eight pounds, she buys a couple more fat-lady muumuu style dresses. Except for her morning walk, Janet's pattern is the same, she starves all day, then eats most of her 1200 calories at night -- eating directly from the refrigerator while she stands by it. When a man she likes pays her a compliment, she panics and blows her diet with a midnight binge. She is basically "willpowering" this diet, and it will not work!

Janet's fate is typical of all those who go on any kind of 'diet-type' behavior --
whether the problem is food, drugs, etc. The "white knuckle' approaches to solving
problems centering around unhealthy habits are short term and ineffective. If you are hoping
to conquer problems related to your unhealthy habit, you must look toward PERMANENT
CHANGES IN YOUR LIFE! Obviously, those changes must be ones that you can live with
comfortably. In fact, I TRULY BELIEVE THAT YOU WILL NOT BE SECURE IN A
NEW LIFESTYLE UNTIL YOU HAVE FOUND A WAY TO ENJOY THE RESULTS OF
YOUR CHANGES, MORE THAN YOU ENJOY THE IMMEDIATE GOOD FEELINGS
PRODUCED BY YOUR UNHEALTHY HABIT! It is important for you to keep looking and
not lose heart. You WILL find rewards in terms of greater self-esteem and self-confidence,
achievements you wouldn't want to give up for any price including a "just one more time"
fling with your old unhealthy lifestyle habit.

An unhealthy habit is rather like driving an old car that always pulls to the left.
When you first begin to change, and you are highly motivated at the beginning of a new
program, you will be sure to hold tightly to the steering wheel to keep yourself going straight
ahead.

The good news is that unlike a car which will always veer left until you have it
repaired, a human being who goes "straight" long enough will eventually adapt to the
change, for after a while, "straight" becomes normal. The bad news is that until this
adaptation takes place, or when the novelty of the program wears off and we are confronted
with various forms of stress, we tend to let go of the wheel -- and there we are, veering off
to the left of the road again, just like the car.

Strong structures keep you on the right road.

So, how can we stay with it long enough to teach ourselves to go straight on a permanent basis? It's a sure bet that over time we will have emotional upsets, social or career disappointments, and a load of temptations. The only way to stay on track during rough times is to construct barriers (structures) for ourselves, much like the ones that keep amusement park bumper cars in line. Even when we let go of the steering wheel, the track forces the car to bounce back to the center, and keep going. These external structures force us to stay on the "straight and narrow."

As we all know, motivation comes easy at first. After the initial rush of good intentions fizzles in the wake of trying times, you are going to need as many external structures as you can create to compensate for the ebb and flow of internal motivations. If it is a good structure it will force you to go straight long enough for your new behavior to become normal and ultimately more rewarding than your unhealthy habits.

Remember, structures need to be built while your motivation is elevated; so when your energy or motivation wears down, the system you have developed will carry you forward. Don't wait until you need the structures to get through the next few hours. Start building them today!

JEFF'S STORY, "BUILDING STRUCTURES"

Jeff, being a very shy young man, was introduced to cocaine by his friends. To his amazement, his social weaknesses seemed to go away when he was under the influence. When Jeff got high he had no problem asking girls out for dates or enjoying himself at parties. However, over time, his drug use increased until he found himself living in the "cocaine lifestyle." Not only did he compulsively use cocaine every weekend, but he began to replace his old true friendships with new drug culture companions. Even when he decided

Structures come in all shapes and sizes.

to go "straight," and kick the habit, his new drug-friends would call him every Friday to see if he "needed anything." Since the girls he had been dating also used, Jeff found it very difficult to get through the weekend without cocaine or a social life. Together, he and I sat down and designed a number of structures to help him create positive replacements in all areas of his life.

First, we decided that Jeff would probably find it easier to stay away from drugs if his so-called "good friends" didn't call him and offer to help him get drugs every Friday night. This was done by informing certain acquaintances that the police would be contacted should he ever receive another call from them. We also decided he should change his telephone number to an unlisted one. Other friends, who would just 'drop by' and have the drugs with them, wanted to stay at Jeff's house and 'party' all night long with other fiends they could invite to join them. Jeff "took the bull by the horns" in this situation, and with great courage told them that under no circumstances would they be welcome at his house again. Lastly, Jeff and I developed a whole series of activities that he could engage in on a regular basis, all of which were totally incompatible with drug use and 'getting high.' This not only included joining team sports, and a support group that appealed to Jeff, but it also meant taking classes to learn how to achieve confidence and verbal fluency that would make him socially acceptable with people other than the drug-using crowd.

What we had done was build structures for Jeff. Even with these structures, the work was difficult and there was much more to accomplish before he felt stabilized in his new life. Jeff was once again putting five fingers down on the table, one at a time, to regain his normal stability. These structures forced Jeff to realize and then to act on the fact that he still had difficulty in the social and sexual arena, and in dealing with loneliness, boredom, and mood regulation without the use of cocaine. But, the structures were the first phase of creating a progressive lifestyle change. If he had relied strictly on initial motivation, he surely would still be using drugs today. I can also assure you that during the months of his transformation he let go of the wheel many times. The bottom line for Jeff was that he created enough healthy structures to carry him forward during difficult times until his new life brought him more joy than his old one ever had.

CREATING YOUR OWN STRUCTURES

In the famous movie "Gone With The Wind" when the main character, Scarlet O'Hara faced a difficult situation, she usually would postpone any action on it by saying "Tomorrow is another day, I'll think about it tomorrow." The same excuse could apply to you: "Tomorrow is another day, I'll stop tomorrow" -- OR -- "I'll begin my new life tomorrow."

There are a thousand and one tomorrows and they are all only a day away, but TODAY IS THE TIME TO TAKE CONTROL! You have made your decision to build new structures for yourself. It wasn't an easy decision, but your decision is worthless unless you commit yourself to action today! There is an old rhyme that applies very well here, perhaps if you memorize it -- it can be of use to you in the future when you are about to postpone taking proper action for developing healthy habits. It goes like this:

> "I've only got a minute-
>
> There's only 60-seconds in it-
>
> I didn't choose it-
>
> But, I can't refuse it-
>
> So, it's up to me to use it-
>
> Do It Now! -- Do It Now! -- Do It Now!

BACKGROUND

As you go about building structures, keep in mind that there are two broad groups of habits that need to be understood because of their similarities. The two groups are "Sedating Habits" and "Stimulating Habits." Let's take a closer look at the SEDATING HABITS:

- Alcohol

- Marijuana

- Tranquilizers

- Sleeping Medications

- Heroin and other morphine derivatives

- Pain Killers

- Laziness

- Lack of Concentration (day dreaming, fantasizing, escape from reality, etc.)

- Bad Work Habits

- Certain types of Food (rich sauces, cookies, ice cream, cakes, bread, etc.)

- Certain types of Relationships (associating with negative, non-motivated people, sitting around with 'pot-smoking' friends, associating with people who make laziness a lifestyle, etc.)

- Television (escapism through total concentration on television)

- Worry (constant concern and worry about everything)

- Passivity and Withdrawal

- Procrastination and Failure

- Laxatives

You should remember from our prior discussion in this book, that people who engage in sedating habits prefer to feel calm rather than stimulated. People at the "Sedating" end of

You should remember from our prior discussion in this book, that people who engage in sedating habits prefer to feel calm rather than stimulated. People at the "Sedating" end of the spectrum are trying to block out emotions. They think that if they can distance themselves enough from reality and life's situations, this will act as insulation from the many uncomfortable and perhaps threatening situations with which they would have to normally cope. So, if you fall into this category, you need to recognize all the factors that apply to your type so that you can arm yourself with the proper tools.

If you have been seeking short-cut methods of sedation, you will now need to spend extra energy thinking of activities that will calm and relax you. Healthy things such as hot tubs, meditation, yoga, biofeedback, self-hypnosis, and soothing music are just some of the avenues you can take to avoid returning to your unhealthy quick-fix, while maintaining a firm hold on reality and all of its problems and challenges.

The primary appeal of all sedating habits is that they enable you to maintain a low arousal level. One of your long-term goals will be to learn to tolerate higher levels of stimulation. While practicing the relaxation techniques, you will need to re-label as normal those levels which you now consider anxiety-producing and undesirable.

Now, let's look at the STIMULATING HABITS:

- Diet Pills
- Amphetamines
- Thrill-seeking Activities (hang gliding, rock climbing, para-sailing, etc.)
- Cocaine and other related drugs
- Workaholism and Stress Addiction
- Compulsive Exercise

- Sex

- Pornography

- Gambling

- Compulsive Shopping and Spending

- Anger

- Sports (excessively playing, watching, or focusing on)

- Video Games

- Caffeine (coffee, tea, soft drinks, chocolate, etc.)

- Shoplifting and Stealing

- Violence

- Criminal activities (breaking the rules, breaking laws)

- Cigarette Smoking

People at the "Stimulating" end of the spectrum are basically running away from their emotions. This group of people thinks that if you are manic enough and run fast enough, you can stay away from the feelings long enough to avoid discomfort and anxiety. This type of person finds that their habits make them quite an expert in this area.

What you need to do now is to find new non-destructive methods to replace your short-cuts. Things such as computer games, loud music, competitive sports -- anything that will keep your arousal level naturally high -- are useful if not used to excess. At the same time, you must learn to tolerate LOWER levels of arousal. Typically, you have labeled such feeling states as "Boredom." Now, you must learn to consider them as acceptable, rather than something you need to escape from or fix. At first, you may feel empty and very uncomfortable, but a certain amount of boredom is a natural part of the human experience. In time, what once seemed intolerable will begin to feel normal.

YOUR TOOL BOX

In building structures, you need the right tools for the job. The personal calendar is essential; it is the first step and it is the only way you can really become aware of Why, When and How you are "pulling to the left." It will enable you to determine exactly what forces, persons, and conditions are influencing your return to addiction.

By using a personal calendar you will begin to see your lifestyle patterns. You might begin to observe that you do well controlling yourself all day long, but find that after work you feel you deserve a 'reward' of some sort, or a way to wind down which leads you into your bad habit. It becomes clear to you that you need to focus on this area. Instead of being flexible (which means leaving yourself open to temptation) at this early stage of change, you need to make a strong commitment -- not merely "not to engage in your bad habit," but to the PURSUIT OF HEALTHY ACTIVITIES THAT ARE INCONSISTENT WITH YOUR UNHEALTHY BEHAVIORS.

If your Friday nights have been spent dining or 'partying' or even attending events where you are tempted to indulge in your bad habit, you will need to make a 180-degree change. You might join a volleyball team, not just as a member, but as an Equipment Manager who is obligated to show up before the game starts, every time, and in great shape. A lot of people are depending on you to have things in readiness before the game begins. Commit yourself 'to the hilt,' and commit yourself to as many people as possible -- create obligations that you cannot ignore. Box yourself in -- this will protect you from your old negative impulses.   You will find that your self-esteem, health, relationships and often even your economic status will improve.

Allow yourself as little time as possible to stand at the crossroads and think. Tell your friends and family what you are doing and what you are intending to accomplish. Also ask them not to 'correct' or to 'remind' you, like a warden or a jailer. Build new structures and burn all bridges connecting you and your old way of life. Own this project and take responsibility for its construction -- for you are the primary beneficiary!

So, today, go down to your local stationary store and buy yourself a year calendar/datebook. Not one that you put on the wall with the picture on it, but a small one that can you carry around with you on a daily basis. Try to find one that gives you room to write things in at different hours of the day, such as one that gives you a whole page or a vertical column for each day. Avoid the ones that just give you a little box for the whole day. Also, see if you can find one that is segmented by the hour or even the half hour.

Next, with a black pen, make a detailed schedule of your typical week. Indicate what time you normally get up, when you eat, what hours you work, and the time allowed for errands, social events, sleep, leisure, etc. Be very thorough and do not omit any details of your day.

Now, take a red pen and note the 'Prime Times' for your bad habits or unhealthy behavior. For example, perhaps you count calories all day but tend to 'clean out the refrigerator' late at night, or perhaps the weekend is your time to really devote a major block of your time to indulging in your unhealthy habits. Whatever pattern your habits follow, indicate the hours in as detailed a manner as is possible.

The next step is to use a green pen and go back to wherever you have red-lined hours or minutes, reschedule, as best as you can, those times with specific activities that you must do. Be systematic and try to burn old bridges completely as you integrate the new behavior into your lifestyle.

When you are finished with this exercise, commit yourself to doing this type of scheduling for at least the next year or two - or even longer. Each and every week, fill in what appointments you have, social events, lunch/dinner dates, etc. Don't forget to schedule in each week when you are going to fill in this calendar for the following week. If you are resisting doing this, then it is exactly the correct tool for you to use. It has been my experience that some people are notoriously late, forgetful, or resistant to structures of any kind. You may be fighting an old battle here from your childhood. This time-structuring activity definitely is not to be looked upon by you as being like Mom or Dad telling you to do 'this or that.' This is only you, helping yourself follow through with what you have committed yourself to do -- develop healthy habits. The sooner you start taking control of your time and activities, the sooner you will be free of your unhealthy habits and in control of your life once again. As an important side benefit, if you follow YOUR schedule, you won't miss important appointments, and therefore you will not find yourself overwhelmed with guilt and worry because you didn't do something. Be nice to yourself -- your life is complex enough already, so don't rely on your memory exclusively. You need to put things down on paper, make lists, and keep your 'thinking energy' for problem solving situations during the day. Not wasting your mind's energy holding small facts, or dates and times, frees you for better thinking. Lastly, and most importantly, use this calendar, carry it with you wherever you go. Refer to it often and add to it often. It is YOUR tool -- USE IT!!

WHAT DO YOU DO WITH YOUR TIME?

Week of:_____ (Day)

	SUN	MON	TUES	WED	THURS	FRI	SAT
6:00am							
6:30							
7:00							
7:30							
8:00							
8:30							
9:00							
9:30							
10:00							
10:30							
11:00							
11:30							
noon							
12:30							
1:00							
1:30							
2:00							
2:30							
3:00							
3:30							
4:00							
4:30							
5:00							
5:30							

WHAT DO YOU DO WITH YOUR TIME?

Week of:_____ (Night)

	SUN	MON	TUES	WED	THURS	FRI	SAT
6:00pm							
6:30							
7:00							
7:30							
8:00							
8:30							
9:00							
9:30							
10:00							
10:30							
11:00							
11:30 mid-night							
12:30							
1:00							
1:30							
2:00							
2:30							
3:00							
3:30							
4:00							
4:30							
5:00							
5:30							

FOCUS ON IMMEDIATE SHORT TERM DAILY ACTIVITIES

While analysis and philosophizing have their place, the first few months of bad habit breaking are not the time for introspection. At this point in time, 'asking why' will only waste your energy, and perhaps put you in touch with feelings that will make your task even more difficult. Right now, it is imperative that you fill your new calendar so that nothing is left to chance. Force yourself to go blindly forward, developing a sort of protective tunnel-vision that will keep you moving ahead and able to ignore temptations. Fill your calendar and follow the schedule! Allow yourself as little time to think as possible!

As we have discussed before, many of the so-called cravings you will experience as you push forward are not indications of physical longings as much as a need to fill a vacuum. That's why unplanned hours and passive activities should be avoided. In their place, plan your days as specifically as possible and allow yourself no time to drift.

Here are some samplings of activities you may wish to consider as you create your own structures:

- Some people can 'go it alone,' while others find support groups helpful. If you require a support group, choose the one that meets your needs as much as possible. Do not join a group and force yourself to conform to them. Some that are available for consideration are: Rational Recovery, Secular Organizations for Sobriety, Women for Sobriety, Weight Watchers, and all 12 step meetings such as Alcoholics Anonymous, Overeaters Anonymous, Cocaine Anonymous, Emotions Anonymous, Alanon, or Co-Dependent Groups.

- Church or Synagogue activities.

- Sign-up for classes which include adult night school, extension courses, drama or writing workshops, pottery making, stained glass window making, sports lessons, etc.

- Movie or theatre outings with friends.

- Attend gallery openings.

- Join a club for sailing, stamp collecting, poetry reading, craft making, etc.

- Get involved with politics and political fund raising activities.

- Do volunteer work for Public Television, delivering meals to the disabled, reading for the blind, stuffing envelopes, tutoring, working the door at events, etc.

- Participate in team sports such as baseball, bowling, volleyball, or soccer.

- Make dates to meet friends at health food restaurants.

- Attend auctions (unless you are a compulsive shopper).

- Run errands or spend time with elderly or disabled people.

- Start jogging or weight training, etc.

- Get together with beneficial friends as often as possible.

- If you play a musical instrument, join a band.

- Take up hobbies such as gardening, painting, stamp collecting, model building, coin collecting, etc.

- Make plans to be with supportive people, do not isolate yourself.

- Take a brief vacation to a health resort.

- Have something sweet and sugar free in the house at all times.

- Restore old cars or antique furniture.

- Volunteer to help at the local hospital, clinic, or school.

It doesn't matter which activities you choose as long as they provide a source of enjoyment for you (you should really like what you do) as they help you create new structures. However, try to devise structures that make it as difficult as possible for you to engage in the unhealthy habit. This means often not just attending a support group, but volunteering to be the secretary and having some responsibility in the meeting. Lock yourself in to these healthy structures, because your motivation WILL weaken and you will need your structures to keep you going forward in spite of what your head is telling you. One last point, structures that involve other people are always better than structures you do by yourself.

There are some powerful outside forces connected with every unhealthy habit. Not only must you cope with the seductive feeling of the habit itself, but you're going to have to tackle a whole array of attendant social and behavioral forces.

Unhealthy habits involve more than merely a physical/emotional dependency on a particular substance or behavior pattern. We also become reliant on expending our energy and time in a way that involves a variety of people, places, and things. After years of interacting with us, the people in our daily lives have come to expect us to behave in certain ways, and in turn, many of their actions are in direct response to ours. Simply, in order to successfully change ourselves, we must either change or resist our external environment.

If you cannot resist the old social pressures, then you must come to terms with the need to move to something new. Replacing old friends with new ones who share your new lifestyle is a sensitive matter and a decision you will have to make in your best interest as you go along. If you don't wish to cut all ties, you can keep in touch with these friends on a limited basis, via the telephone or with an occasional lunch.

If your problem is filling up those long evening hours, you are going to need a number of new acquaintances who enjoy the same kind of lifestyle that you are trying to achieve. You meet these new friends at work, in church, or in the new groups and activities that you have just joined. By carefully rescheduling your time in a new and creative way to include whatever support you can muster, you will endow yourself with additional leverage in your favor.

THE ESCAPE HATCH

Whenever your body tempts you to return to familiar habits, whenever it sabotages you by veering to the left, you will need to have an escape hatch handy. Make a list of reliable friends that you can call or items you can pull out of a drawer to quickly divert your attention. Some useful escape hatches are as follows:

- If you are giving up smoking cigarettes, such simple replacements as a toothpick, rubber band or paperclip can be used to occupy your hands. Literally anything that keeps you from reaching for a cigarette will do. Some of my clients have found that playing video games keeps them well occupied and away from old habits. The main thing is not to give yourself time to think.

- If you are a shopacholic, don't keep your credit cards in your wallet or purse. Painful though it might be, put them in the bank safe deposit box, or if that doesn't work, cut them up with scissors.

- If food is your unhealthy habit of choice, toss out the box of cookies or cake mix. Pack the high-fat items such as crackers, nuts, baked goods, cheese, and sour cream in a box and donate them to your favorite homeless shelter, mission, or charity. Keep the house empty of all foods that contribute to your unhealthy habit. If you are going to slip, make it as difficult as possible for yourself. Replace all the high-fat foods with low-fat substitutes such as fat-free frozen ice cream and yogurt, fruits, sweet vegetables, and rice. They will fill up your emptiness and help you resist destructive "spur of the moment" cravings. Always keep your kitchen cabinets and refrigerator full of low-cal, healthy food -- have something sugar-free and sweet in the house at all times.

- If your unhealthy habit involves a "group or pack" mentality, such as doing drugs, or bar-hopping with friends, tell those people well ahead of time that you are not available and make sure no one just happens to 'drop by.'

If you can't make it impossible to pursue your habit, at least make it difficult to indulge. Give yourself a break by giving your unhealthy habits NO break at all! BURN THOSE BRIDGES RIGHT NOW!

THE OVERALL STRATEGY

During the first phase of change, we must prepare to spend a great amount of energy to attain our goals and resist temptation. Most experts would agree that it is best to attack only one unhealthy habit at a time. Tackling a compulsive eating disorder while becoming a non-smoker may be admirable, but it is really a tough order to fill. The same is true with alcohol and drug use. However, in this case there is a significant 'if.' If you can cut out your drug use while keeping your alcohol intake moderate (one or two drinks a day maximum), then that's the way to go. But, if you find that using cocaine or tranquilizers causes you to compensate with extra alcohol intake, there is little choice but to stop both habits at once.

Even though your ultimate goal may be to modify your habit, I recommend that you abstain completely for a minimum of two or three months (unless your unhealthy habit involves a chemical or behavior that you must engage in -- like taking medication or eating). Both scientific research and personal experience shows that this strategy gives you the best chance for success.

I think this book will teach you how to achieve and maintain control throughout your life. The answer is, IT WILL, if you first learn how not to need your habit at all. This is a simple fact, but very important to understand.

The longer you stay away from the quick-fix, the more healthy strategies you will create for yourself, and therefore, the less likely you will be to return to your unhealthy habits. During the time you are abstinent, you will be forced to develop a variety of internal and external coping skills that will help you handle all kinds of feelings, thoughts, and behaviors.

Your goal is to get comfortable within a 24-hour period without engaging in your unhealthy habit. Get comfortable with the new activities that you develop which take up the vacuum that was left when you 'walked-away' from your unhealthy habit.

For example, if you have been drinking heavily, a period of abstinence should force you to develop coping skills to overcome boredom, frustration, and bad moods, while managing stress. You must develop new ways of spending your time in a satisfying and fulfilling manner. If you think that these abilities are not necessary, you are very wrong -- you need them to help hold off the old destructive habits.

It is so important that you allow yourself enough time to learn these needed skills. You will not master them quickly, and you will never learn them at all if you are still turning to the old excuses when the going gets rough. Only when you feel that you have a variety of other well-practiced ways of dealing with difficulties should you even think of attempting moderation. For your habit should never again hold center stage, or be relied upon as a methodology of choice. Rather, it should be just one of many methods, only one of perhaps 25 support fingers; something you can choose to forgo in place of healthier lifestyle choices.

Initiating new behavior is never easy, and replacing unhealthy habits with productive activities is a major challenge. While a positive attitude is desirable, it is wise not to underestimate your task. Those who envision a too-rosy picture may crumble the first few times they crash into the hard wall of reality. It is vital that you respect the power of the unhealthy habit that you are trying to change. As Newton's Law shows, once a ball is in motion, it will keep rolling until it collides with an outside force or becomes the victim of friction and slowly rolls to a dead stop.

What you are actively doing now is forcing the "old ball" (your unhealthy habits) to go in a brand new direction (your new healthy habits).

THE GETAWAY

In order to give yourself a head start those first few difficult days, it is smart to schedule a brief vacation. It could be a weekend or a week. By going outside your normal environment and changing your scenery, you can gain an immediate edge. If you are married or in a relationship, invite your significant other along (unless they are part of the problem), and fill your vacation calendar with numerous specific activities. As always, active rather than passive activities will keep you not only occupied but challenged. Resorts that offer tennis, golf, swimming, scuba diving, or horseback riding will make positive demands on your energy and help keep boredom away.

I AM WHAT I SEE, I AM WHERE I WANT TO BE

Visualization techniques have been used in so many areas that it is now practically a household term. From fighting disease to upping work production to psyching out tennis opponents, visualization is an accessible and viable tool in actualizing goals.

Here's how it can work for you: several days or even several weeks before the appointed day when you give up your unhealthy habit, start picturing yourself going about your life without practicing your habit. Create detailed plots and write the scripts now. If, you are constantly making jokes about yourself or keeping romantic advances at bay with layers of fat, imagine how differently you will behave when you are thin. Visualize yourself accepting compliments as you shed your weight, and think about how you will handle and welcome the positive aspects of your new healthy habit lifestyle. It just may seem a little scary to you at first because all these plots may be new territory for you. So practice now, see yourself as a new self -- hear your new self speaking -- let yourself feel how your new life is going to be.

For example, if your problem is with cigarettes, visualize yourself at a party or at your office. How are you going to stand there and keep talking without your cigarette in hand? What can you say or do to pull yourself away from the work task or conversation without running to put a cigarette in your mouth? What could you reply when someone comments about you not smoking or offers you a cigarette. What can you mentally tell yourself when the conversation gets heated or when you feel lonely, other than, "I need a cigarette?"

Personally, I found this technique particularly helpful, as a means to begin to classify or identify myself as a non-smoker, or a non-drinker, or a non-drug user, etc. What I mean is that our bad habits are part of us and we often define and see ourselves as a smoker, drinker, or drug user. I suggest that you visualize yourself as a person who doesn't participate in these unhealthy habits. Create a mental picture of what a non-smoker does. How do non-smokers communicate with people, how do they take breaks, what do they do after a meal, how do that go from room to room at home and at the office without a cigarette as a prop, how do they handle being alone, and how do they handle stressful and crisis situations at home and at work. It is very important to start getting comfortable with a new definition of yourself and a new identity for yourself, and this is the first and safest way to do that.

TRY AND TRY AGAIN

Many people get discouraged when they try to conquer a habit and fail. If that happens to you, don't become depressed and disheartened. How many friends do you know who honestly quit smoking the very first time they tried? How many people do you know who are on the diet cycle of losing and gaining it back?

The truth is, the more times you attempt something, the better your chances are at succeeding the next time you try. Just like learning to swim or ride a bicycle, it takes many attempts before you realize success. With each subsequent try, you 'go into the ring' with more muscle, more skills, and more understanding. We do learn from our mistakes and that knowledge wises us up and makes us tougher. Don't let yourself fall into the "I'm a

Failure" trap! Pick yourself up, ask the important questions about what happened to cause the slip and then get moving forward again. As we have said before, learn from what works, but also learn from what doesn't work.

When you have one of those days when you feel that you "just can't handle it," think about how you feel when you dive into a cold swimming pool on a hot day. At first, the shock of the cold water on your hot skin is extremely unpleasant, but if you stay in the pool for about three to five minutes, you find that the water temperature is suddenly more pleasant. You then swim and have a good time. However, if you had gotten out of the pool because of those first uncomfortable minutes, you would have missed an enjoyable and relaxing swim in the pool. If you can just "sit with it" (just bear those unpleasant feelings and emotions for a little while), the bad feelings will start to decrease and you will find that you are regaining control of your natural coping skills.

Remember, when you are wrestling with unhealthy habits, if you don't experience discomfort comparable to diving into a cold pool, then you're missing something. Productive change is never easy or comfortable. If there was such a thing as a 'magic bullet' that could be shot into you which would immediately remove your unhealthy habit, every shop in the nation would stock them. So, embrace those pangs and failures of transition, and know that they are evidence of progress -- the surest sign of growth and control.

STOP, IN THE NAME OF LOVE?

While you think that it is admirable to give up an unhealthy habit to please a spouse, lover, friends or relatives you really don't have a very good chance of accomplishing attaining that goal. If you, yourself, are not ready, really ready, to dump the bad habit because you want to in your heart of hearts, then now is not the time. Save all the energy and trouble until you are genuinely motivated. Remember, because someone says to you: "I love you, give up this unhealthy habit for me because you love me," just doesn't work. This is a personal choice that cannot be accomplished in the name of love.

PAUSE-STOP-THINK-REFLECT-VISUALIZE-ACT

We have reached the place in the book where you should pause and put into practice all that we have discussed to this point. Let me repeat, YOU MUST DO WHAT WE HAVE DISCUSSED IN THE BOOK TO THIS POINT!! This will take some time and energy on your part. Instead of going on with the book, please stop, and re-read the vital points of this book that are so important to your development of the healthy habits you want. You now have a whole tool chest that will work for you and enable you to gain control over your unhealthy habits. You must take time to create the strong structures that you need and build the confidence in yourself that will enable you not to slip back into the old patterns. Do not leave this book!! Read it every day! Read the same chapters over and over -- highlight with a yellow marker the most important and relevant parts for you -- and let them be your keys to success.

After you have reached a plateau of success, it is vital that you continue reading this book to cement in the beneficial changes you have made. Now is not the time to go too fast, or the second half of this book will be less effective! Good Luck!

PAUSE HERE!

RE-READ!

TAKE CONTROL NOW!

TAKE CONTROL NOW!

CHAPTER 4 SECRETS FOR SUCCESS

PART 1 THINGS I CAN CONTROL AND MANAGE

"Up from the pastures of boredom

out from the sea of discontent

they come in packs like hungry hounds

the seekers of the dark enchantment."

This quote from Rod McKuen's poem, "The Lovers," captures the mood and feeling that you get when you become discontent, bored, angry, or any one of many different emotional states or situations that you can use to abandon your quest for developing healthy habits and return to the "dark enchantment" of your unhealthy habit. Remember, YOU have the power to change and grow!

If feelings are primary, then the "Pyramid of InterConnections of Life" gives you four directions for attacking the feeling. A plan of attack can be formulated with each point (Social/Environment, BioChemistry, Behavior, and Thinking). In fact, there are a multitude of attack points under each position of the Pyramid -- it is an exponential progression. It synthesizes multiple approaches and it makes sense of why so many methodologies work for so many different people.

THE INTERCONNECTIONS OF LIFE

Please look at the Pyramid diagram. I have developed this in hopes of making some complex inter-relationships easier to understand and use. This four-cornered pyramid lists FEELINGS at the top with each of the four corners of the base represented by the processes of THINKING, BEHAVIOR, SOCIAL/ENVIRONMENT and BIOCHEMISTRY. What I

116

"Pyramid Power"
The Interconnections of Life

am proposing here is that these five life phenomena are significantly interconnected. When you understand exactly how they impact one another, then you will have a powerful set of tools at your disposal.

What we have learned from the F.A.N. concept was that most of our behavior and unhealthy habits are directed toward seeking good feelings and avoiding unpleasant ones. This, of course, suggests that FEELINGS ARE AT THE FOUNDATION OF MOTIVATION, and therefore, have profound control of your lifestyle. What I purposely did not discuss earlier was the definition of feelings and how we can effectively change them. We will address that discussion now.

First, I would like to propose that feelings are nothing more than another feedback system which involves the subjective sensations that we call emotions. They are like our other senses of sight, sound, touch, smell, and taste which also provide feedback on our experiences. As with these other senses, feelings are ultimately produced by bio-chemical changes in our body. When we put salt on our tongue, certain biochemical processes begin instantly sending messages to our brain which determines that it is a taste sensation and the taste is salty. If we look at a picture, the light impacts on the back of our retina, producing a biochemical change which then sends a visual message to our brain. Feelings are simply another sensory system shared by all humans. The crucial point is that we cannot change feelings directly. You cannot say to yourself - "Feel Happy!" - and then expect that your brain will automatically respond. Feelings, those powerful motivators, are always the result of another force. For this reason, they can only be changed indirectly. That is where the pyramid will come into play.

When you are depressed, well-meaning friends often say, "Try to snap out of it -- force yourself to go out and have a good time . . . Feel happy!" Although you may make a valiant attempt at pulling yourself out of the doldrums, you simply cannot change your mood at will. If we could do that, how simple life would be.

The good news is that although we cannot change our feelings directly, we can alter them through a number of indirect methods. Once we understand how to accomplish this, we then have other options besides our unhealthy habits to make ourselves feel better.

The way that we learn to change feelings is by understanding the connected relationships between five interdependent processes:

- Biochemistry

- Behavior

- Thinking

- Feeling

- Social/Environment

When you feel sad, you can't just sit in your living room and suddenly experience a spontaneous change. However, if you get up and jog around the block, the exercise will alter your biochemistry, which in turn will make you feel differently, and those new feelings will affect your thought process.

The same is true if you leave an empty house or office and walk into a lively social scene. Unless you literally stand in a corner staring at the wall, you will be forced to interact with others -- talking, listening and perhaps laughing. This change in social environment, like physical exercise, will impact on your thinking and biochemistry, which in turn will create new thoughts and feelings.

If you have any doubts about the validity of this concept, rest assured that even primates are affected by it. For example, studies show that changes in a male monkey's social environment will actually alter his testosterone level. Depending on the circumstances, he will become either more or less assertive.

In Human Beings, the results are equally direct and sometimes dramatic. When you adopt a more positive view of yourself (a change in thinking), you will no longer let yourself be pushed around (behavioral change), and that will cause your biochemistry to become altered which will make you feel differently, and those new feelings may alter your thoughts and behavior even more. It's all a very complex, dynamic, fluid, interaction between the five components. Each one is constantly in flux, shifting and moving -- changing along with each of the others.

The first step in regaining control of our lives is to have an understanding of those aspects that we can control, and those that we cannot. As we discussed, if we are depressed, it is senseless for someone to simply suggest, "Cheer up!" But, through changes in our behavior, our environment, our biochemistry or our thinking, we can effectively combat this feeling we call Depression. By changing any one of these factors, we can almost immediately gain some degree of control over our emotional states. In other words, if we are sad, a brisk walk, telling ourself different thoughts, an assertive action, a nutritional change or a little risk-taking can help switch us into a better mood.

The following diagram shows a number of possible combinations for these inter-relationships:

- **THINKING:** Affects biochemistry -- which affects feelings

- THINKING: Affects behavior -- which affects biochemistry -- which can alter feelings

- THINKING: Affects biochemistry -- which affects feelings -- which can alter behavior

- BEHAVIOR: Affects thinking -- which affects biochemistry -- which can alter feelings

- BEHAVIOR: Affects social environment -- which affects thinking -- which can alter biochemistry -- which affects feelings

- BEHAVIOR: Affects biochemistry -- which affects feelings

- SOCIAL ENVIRONMENT: Affects behavior -- which affects thinking -- which can alter biochemistry -- which affects feelings

- SOCIAL ENVIRONMENT: Affects thinking -- which affects biochemistry -- which can alter feelings

- FEELINGS: Affect behavior -- which can affect thinking -- which can alter biochemistry -- which affects feelings

- FEELINGS: Affect thinking -- which affects behavior -- which alter biochemistry -- which affects feelings

This is not an all-inclusive list of possible inter-relationships, but rather a starting point to help you use the tools and techniques that will be presented throughout the rest of this book. As you can see, what is involved is a dynamic interaction of life processes that if understood well, can help you achieve maximum control over your life.

If we understand that these four processes (Thinking, Behavior, Social Environment, and Biochemistry) cause Feelings, then we have the understanding and the tools to change and maintain those changes.

DEPRESSION

Depression is a feeling which deserves special attention because it is both common and profound. Mild transient depression affects us all from time to time, but when it becomes prolonged, we call it clinical depression and we attempt to treat it with drugs or psychotherapy or both.

A normal reactive depression resulting from the loss of a job, the chaos of a relationship, or the death of a loved one can become more serious when biochemistry is altered in response to emotions. This is what happened to one of my patients.

JERRY'S STORY

Jerry was in his thirties, married, father of two, and an up-and-coming Certified Public Accountant with a large firm. Many of his clients were heavy-hitters in the Entertainment Industry, giving his work a dimension beyond that of the typical accountant. Competent and secure, Jerry looked forward to further promotions and a bright future.

The only thing in his life that he wanted to change was his smoking habit. The stress of his job prompted him to keep reaching for those cigarettes, to the tune of a pack-a-day. He would quit, but keep going back; that was the price of his fast-track life.

Unfortunately, like many workers/professionals in the early 1990's, he fell victim to the recession. As it took its toll even among the rich and famous, business was significantly cut back at the firm. His employers had no choice but to reduce their staff. Shocked and depressed, Jerry began sending his resume around, while his wife went back to work full time. When he wasn't able to find another position to match the one that he had lost, he began trying smaller, less prestigious firms and was distressed to find that few of them were hiring. After several weeks of hearing that he was overqualified and that his resume would be kept on file, he was reduced to free-lance temporary bookkeeping jobs just to make ends meet.

His depression was understandable and normal. No one in his right mind would be unaffected by such a bleak situation. Jerry's friends also began to influence the way that he thought about himself which affected his behavior. Confidence gave way to insecurity, and eventually insecurity drifted into a sense of worthlessness. Where Jerry had once charmed his friends with stories concerning Hollywood celebrities, he now felt embarrassed, withdrawn and ashamed to talk about his reduced status and income. His feelings of loss were translated into both conscious and unconscious thoughts of: "I'm not good enough." "I'll probably never have that kind of job again."

As Jerry's hopeless thoughts impacted his behavior, his once energetic demeanor slowed to a crawl. In his leisure hours, he replaced social events and sports with television or random activity. His wife tried to be patient, compassionately viewing his negative state as a temporary symptom. At the same time, she was being caught up in her own career demands and job stress. As he felt worse, his cigarette habit increased. As the pain of depression grew, he found himself chain-smoking nearly three packs per day, plus drinking and eating more. Although he found temporary relief in these short-cuts, in actuality, he was causing his depression to deepen.

It wasn't long before the changes in Jerry's behavior resulted in altered biochemistry. His reactive depression was reinforced by chemical changes that caused reduced neurological brain function. That contributed still more to his lethargy, melancholy and lack of motivation. The downward spiral continued, until one day he just didn't get out of bed.

His wife accepted his explanation that he must have a touch of the flu. Then the weekend came and she soon realized that her husband had no fever, no respiratory symptoms, nothing more than general malaise. Fortunately, she acted quickly and decisively. She insisted that he get some counseling -- not soon -- but now!! She didn't ask, she demanded. Prompted by her insistence, he took the first step toward reversing his vicious cycle.

The day that he came to my office, I explained the dynamics of feelings, thinking, behavior, and biochemistry, and how these processes interact with one another in both directions -- positive and negative. In spite of his depression, his sharp intellect and passion for logic enabled him to get a clear view of what was happening to him. Although he didn't even feel like being out of bed, much less quitting smoking and drinking, he was able to recognize how critical these changes were to his recovery.

As he was leaving that afternoon, he told me that he was so tired all he wanted to do was sleep. But, before walking out the door I encouraged him to use my phone to call a friend and set up a game of racket ball. "I'll probably pass out on the court," he said as he left.

In fact, he did not pass out, but made another date for later that very week -- and the next and the next. Although it was possibly the worst time in his life, he cut out the cigarettes, and began eating healthier, and stopped most of his alcohol use. One weekend he accompanied his wife to a dinner party and attended the theatre the next day. He was dragging at first, but his energy gradually returned and his thinking became more optimistic. He plodded along with his free-lance accounts and spent more time socializing, both at parties and at the sports club -- without having to fortify himself with his old bad habits. After a while, instead of hating his new lifestyle, he started to enjoy it and recognize the long-term benefits. In short, he began to feel good again, both physically and mentally.

The point of Jerry's story is to demonstrate that when you understand this concept, you will have tremendous power within your grasp. While in the grip of a downward slide there is no question you will feel hopeless. But once armed with the simple knowledge of how feelings, thoughts, social environments, actions and chemistry interact, you can take definitive steps to harness this dynamic process and make it work for you, rather than against you.

BE CREATIVE

I will be discussing specific strategies based on the Pyramid Mode. The best way to benefit from them is to use them creatively. The creative process is wrought with both excitement and apprehension because it means trying something new and different without any guarantees of success. So, rather than making a particular outcome your goal, it is best to simply aspire toward creativity itself. When you are creative, it is certain you will not stay in the same rut for very long.

Whatever strategies you create for yourself, it is important that you stick with them. Therefore, it makes sense to design activities and practices that are compatible with your own particular lifestyle, taste, and self-image. You can best do this by seeking what I call a 'resonating experience.' Resonating experiences are those experiences which best suit you and are the ones that will help you permanently internalize your mood-altering skills.

For example, if you are in a museum or art gallery, you might see a painting and say "Not bad." Then all of a sudden, you will turn a corner and say, "Wow! That's beautiful!" Meanwhile, the person that you are with might respond, "It's okay, but look over there."

You don't need to figure out why a particular object or experience touches you profoundly, only be aware that it does. Such a reaction indicates a 'resonating experience,' the kind of 'creative happening' you will need to pursue and explore. All too often, we find ourselves responding to other people's expectations or using the tools that work for them rather than going after what feels right for us. That often results in pent-up anger or resentment, and only a short-lived integration of the tool. It is essential that you do it your way and not Mom's, Dad's or anyone else's way. Don't keep boxing up your real needs, instead design and create tools and techniques that feel right to you in a way that is both comfortable and exciting.

Always focus on our motto: "Skill Yourself, Don't Kill Yourself."

TAKE CONTROL NOW!

CHAPTER 4 SECRETS FOR SUCCESS

PART 2 YOUR FEELINGS

"I drown my feelings with work. I just plunge myself into my job and focus on nothing else. I never allow myself time to dwell on myself. I arrive at work early and leave late; and when I do get home, I just drop into bed and sleep and try not to dream."

"I just can't cope with college! It's so different from high school. There are no bells for class changes, the teachers don't take the roll -- they don't care whether you are there or not! The tests are so hard, and the questions don't always come from the book -- you have to take notes and good ones! The teachers call me Mr. Jackson -- I'm used to being called Dave. No one knows me here, and it's so hard to make friends. Even the sign on the locker room door reads MEN and not BOYS like in high school! I'm just over my head. I don't know which way to turn or what to do. I'm just no good . . . I'd like to die."

"I've done this so long, it just seems normal to me. After work, I go home and turn on the TV and turn the sound all the way down. Then I turn on the stereo real loud and I stare at the TV and listen to the music and eat all night long. I start out with a salad and I plan to stop there, but I can't stop. I just live in that kitchen all night cooking and eating. I know this sounds weird, but like I say, it's normal to me. Funny though, I don't know why I act like that, except when I'm doing it, I don't think about anything but the music, the pictures on TV, and the food."

"I dropped out of acting class at school because the professor told us that in order to be a good actor, we had to know ourselves first. I don't want to know myself. I took the class so that I could learn to pretend that I was other people."

Did you ever wonder, as I did some years ago, why nearly all therapists insist that you need to get in touch with your feelings? You might be asking, "What does this have to do with my problem? What is all this feeling mumbo-jumbo anyway? It seems like a lot to ask in addition to giving up my habit!" The simple fact is, we want to identify our feelings so that we can express them in clear simple sentences, so that we can understand how they motivate us and drive us to do certain things, so we can take the steps to gain control. This may be the first time that you have ever understood your feelings, and realized that your feelings are driving your unhealthy habits. Knowledge is power, courage is overcoming fear, and facing our true feelings without fear, gives us the knowledge and power to manage them. It is sometimes difficult to do this, because to come to know our feelings, we often need to rebel against both our personal and cultural upbringing.

A NATIONAL CURSE

We have all seen foreign films where a pair of Italian men embrace each other, weeping and greeting each other shamelessly. While such a scene may seem perfectly natural when viewed above the subtitles of a film, such an encounter on a Seattle or Kansas City street corner would surely raise the eyebrows of passersby. We Americans as a group, and our men especially, are not very comfortable with raw emotions. We resist exploring our feelings, and more often than not, refuse to even acknowledge them.

The more that you guard your emotions, the more you need to learn to bury your feelings. The deeper you bury them, the less and less in touch with yourself you become. Not only are you putting up barriers between yourself and others, you are also putting up barriers between you and your most basic innermost instincts. This is emotional suicide, and leaves you an empty, unresponsive person totally detached from society and family. If you cannot identify or bear your feelings, this is precisely the reason why you are vulnerable to adopting bad habits.

As we have discussed, feelings are the tip of the pyramid. If you are to gain control over your habits, it is obvious that you must first identify the feelings driving the behavior. As you know, feelings that are uncomfortable can be eliminated or avoided by engaging in certain activities; and if those behaviors work, and work well, we tend to repeat them.

It is also true that unhealthy habits are not always an escape from bad feelings. Sometimes, they are a way of seeking out good feelings. In either case, feelings are central to why we continue to repeat certain behaviors even when we know that the short-term rewards will cause long-term damage.

We can easily understand how and why we are motivated to move away from or closer to a particular emotion. If a certain activity -- such as taking a drink -- enables us to quickly and easily feel good, and more comfortable, then that "Elixir" has the potential of becoming a driving force in our life. If we don't consciously know what it is we are feeling -- if we cannot define our emotions well enough to communicate them -- then we are unable to determine what it is that is driving us, and therefore, we will stay in our unhealthy habit routine or on the brink of relapse no matter how hard and long we try to kick the habit.

It may feel comfortable to be numbed out, but it is a dangerous situation any way you look at it. If you were born with no sensors on your fingertips, imagine the burns, cuts and other injuries you would suffer without realizing it. That kind of freedom from physical pain is not a blessing, it is a curse.

There is really no difference where our emotions are concerned. If your emotions and feelings are buried deep within you, when you feel anger and hurt, you won't realize it.

129

You are not going to have the savvy to fix your relationship or confront your boss. If you mellow out with Valium before speaking to a group, you are never going to understand that you need to become more confident and assertive. You will just go blithely on your way, bumping into all kinds of walls, not having a hint as to what is really wrong. Worse of all, you are setting the stage for a lifetime of need for external "Elixirs" (unhealthy habits) as you become more dependent on them -- until finally you require them just to maintain normal function.

We need to understand our feelings because our emotions serve as a compass, guiding and providing us with the feedback to adjust or change, so we can function happily and effectively. This process doesn't evolve overnight, it may even take many years for the necessary self-knowledge and changes to fall into place. Ultimately, if you focus on it long enough, it will happen.

We very much need our emotions to motivate us. If we have been relieving boredom with food, shopping, overwork, alcohol, drugs, or any other quick fix, we have not learned to face and resolve our feelings in a healthful and permanent manner. I realize that it will be very uncomfortable at first, but if you stay with your feelings long enough, they will cause you to deal with them in some way. If you numb your feelings, they will only return at some later time, and you will not have developed any skills or strategies for coping with your feelings. Like it or not, if you are bored long enough, you will eventually join a club, start a new hobby, make new friends and in some way truly resolve those restless feelings. If you are angry with your spouse and you dodge the issue with a short-cut fix, the anger will remain and become more potent and toxic. If you stay with the feeling long enough, you will finally be compelled to sit down and have that long postponed talk. Your task now is to allow all your uncomfortable sensations to work for you.

Let me emphasize again, especially to all of you who pride yourselves on being rational/logical thinkers -- this is not an intellectual process. We indulge again and again in our substances and behaviors because of emotions. Unhealthy habits are nothing more than an over-reliance on one narrow strategy for coping with feelings.

As we learned in The Five Finger Exercise, when a substance or behavior is used as an exclusive means of coping with all your assorted feelings, other skills tend to collapse, leaving us hopelessly unbalanced. It might be a good idea to review The Five Finger Exercise now. I understand how uncomfortable this emotional battle within yourself can be in the beginning, because I have been there too. Believe me, the rewards are very much worth the effort!

The first important distinction that I want to make about feelings is that they are all 'singular words.' I can't tell you how many times I have asked a client, "How do you feel today?" In response, I will get ten long sentences about something related to a feeling. Such as, "I feel she doesn't like me because of X,Y,Z reason." It is important as you learn about feelings, that you ask yourself every day "How do I feel?" and if what comes back in reply is more than one word, then it is a THOUGHT and not a FEELING. So, stop yourself and try to refocus on the subjective sensations inside and try to express it in a single word.

Most of my clients who practice unhealthy lifestyle management habits fail Elementary Emotions. When I ask them, "How do you feel about life?" or "How did you feel when your boss passed you over for the promotion?" -- I get either blank looks or vague

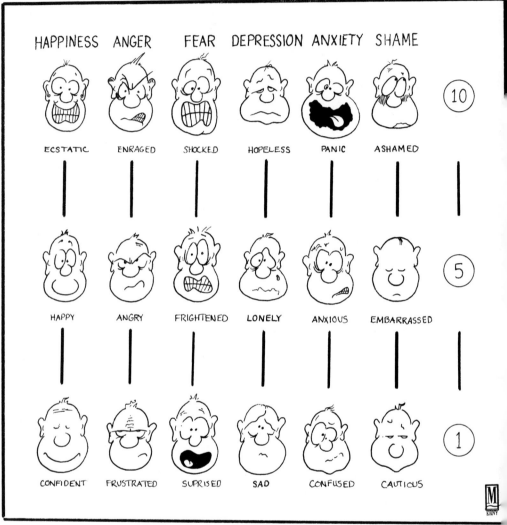

The One-To-Ten's of Emotions

answers. What I teach them, and what I hope you will learn to do, is to put a word to the event -- which simply means learning to call a feeling -- a feeling.

This may sound simple, but it is not mastered in one attempt. It is a skill, much like riding a bicycle or learning to roller skate. It takes much time, patience, and practice. In taking this important step now, namely understanding how you feel, you will come to recognize that feelings are not absolutes, but instead they emerge in various shades and degrees. Most of us, in learning about emotions, were never taught that feelings are not just black or white, happy or sad, angry or content. Emotions exist in many shades of gray.

Most people who are involved in practicing unhealthy habits are notoriously unaware of their feelings, especially the smaller, more subtle feelings. It is this inability to perceive shades of gray which poses a serious barrier to self-understanding and self control. You must pay attention to the subtler events in your life, such as a friend forgetting your birthday, your mother's criticism, or a letter which suddenly lifts your spirits.

Sometimes when I ask a client how he/she feels, the answer will be "tired," or "excited." Those words indicate arousal, not emotion, and the two states are quite different. Arousal is a component of emotion. It indicates the level of excitement -- the degree of energy, exhilaration, or fatigue which you register at any point in time. It is important to realize that certain emotions, like Joy and Anger have high arousal components while Boredom, Calmness, and Depression register on the low end. While arousal and emotion overlap, they are two separate phenomena.

After much trial and error, I have found that it is quite difficult to remember to focus on feelings for any length of time. Given that in the course of a day our attention is constantly diverted, I've found that an external queuing device makes the job much easier and faster. The simplest one to use is an inexpensive digital alarm wristwatch that you can pick up at any discount department store. What I want you to do is set the watch to beep once every hour, so that you can keep track of all the many variations of feelings that you have throughout the day.

In any given 24-hour period, you are going to experience an entire array of subtle emotional shifts. The 'beep' of your watch alarm will simply give you a chance to stop for minute and reflect on what exactly you are feeling. For the first week or two, all you need to do is get into the habit of paying attention to your feelings on a regular basis. Then, when you are used to these hourly mood/emotion checks, you can start to keep an on-going record for yourself -- just make a note every time you hear a signal. Similarly, note your arousal level on a scale of 1 to 10 at the sound of each beep.

At the end of the normal day, you should have about 12 to 16 brief notes. At the end of a week, you can start to put the information to use. Being as specific as possible, plot your emotional highs and lows for a seven-day period -- making note of all persons, locations, and activities involved at each checkpoint. On the separate chart, plot your arousal level numbers.

Be sure that you don't make the mistake of labeling thoughts as feelings. Remember one way to make a quick distinction is to keep in mind that feelings can be easily defined with a single word such as: Sad, Happy, Angry, Lonely, Frightened, etc. If you require more than one word to express yourself then you are reaching for a thought and not a feeling. Thoughts are very important too, but they are not the same as feelings.

Because people practicing unhealthy habits have become so good at "stashing and stuffing" their feelings, whenever their feelings do succeed in jumping out, they seem

PAY ATTENTION TO YOUR FEELINGS

HOURLY MOOD/EMOTION CHECK

Date __OCTOBER 2__
Day of the week __THURSDAY__
Week __#3__

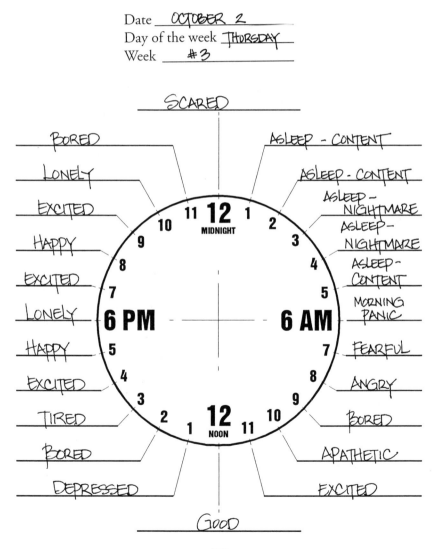

135

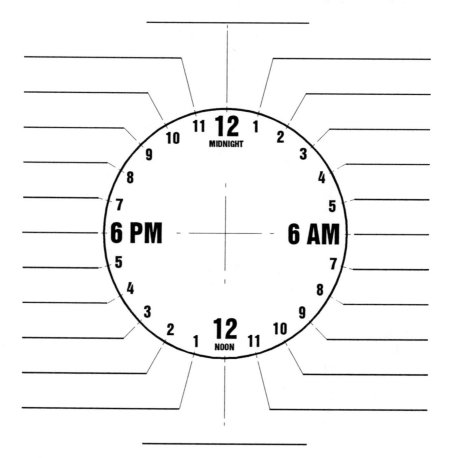

nothing less than overwhelming and terrifying, like nightmares -- instead of being the good and familiar friends they should be. Only through objectivity can we learn to handle and analyze them like a pebble in our hand.

Perhaps, like many of us, you have been told that there are certain emotions that you shouldn't feel, let alone express. Perhaps you grew up in a family where feelings were labeled as 'good' or 'bad,' with the 'bad' feelings being totally off-limits. I had a female client once who remembered from her childhood becoming jealous "when the new little blond girl in school flirted with her fourth grade boyfriend." At home that night, she vocalized her jealousy with all the passion of an uninhibited nine year old, saying, "I hate Sally, for talking to Bobby. He's my friend -- not hers!" Her expression of honest emotion was quickly suppressed by an anxious mother who admonished: "Nice little girls don't talk that way!" Even more dramatic, are examples from children who were reared in alcoholic homes, where the message was just: "Don't feel."

The bottom line is that feelings are just feelings, nothing more. The feelings of anger and even hatred are no worse than love and gratitude. But you still may wonder if certain emotions should be repressed. If no one acted in anger or hatred, we would have no murders and no wars. "Don't fool yourself!" In the world in which we live, when we start roping off half our emotions, we soon forget how to embrace our remaining emotions. Any man, woman or child who 'sits on his anger' is soon going to have a hard time 'letting go with spontaneous joy' or spontaneous anything! Feelings are interconnected, and it is impossible to shut down one without discouraging them all.

In order to help you get started with identifying your feelings, I have listed below some of the major emotions and their manifestations. Remember, if it takes more than a

FEELINGS ARE A MATTER OF DEGREE

	HAPPINESS	DEPRESSION	ANGER	FEAR
SUBTLE **The 1-2-3's of a feeling**	Relieved Refreshed Glad Pleased Amused Content Optimistic Calm Composed Comfortable Cool Secure Relaxed Confident	Flat Bored Discontented Resigned Apathetic Numb Blue Gloomy Low Sad Down Bewildered Blah Melancholy	Peeved Bugged Annoyed Ruffled Harassed Irritated Irked Frustrated Put-upon Resentful	Shy Startled Uneasy Tense Concerned Timid Apprehensive Cautious Pensive Up-tight
MODERATE **The 4-5-6-7's of a feeling**	Delighted Joyful Merry Tickled Glowing Festive Frisky Spry Happy Proud Joyous Excited Cheerful Giddy Great Playful	Disappointed Slighted Drained Disheartened Hurt Ashamed Depressed Lost Regretful Ignored Burdened Rotten Lonely Unhappy Distressed Forlorn	Disgusted Ticked-off Mad Smoldering Riled Pissed-off Hot Contemptuous Animosity Jealous Fed-up Mean Spiteful Angry	Alarmed Jittery Scared Frightened Fearful Threatened Trembly Shaken Anxious Worried Nervous Afraid
INTENSE **The 8-9-10's of a feeling**	Elated Ecstatic Blissful Sparkling Overjoyed Radiant Wonderful Fantastic Exhilarated Enthralled	Miserable Crushed Helpless Humiliated Worthless Abandoned Overwhelmed Hopeless Lifeless Dead	Enraged Fuming Burning-up Furious Incensed Infuriated Destructive Hate-filled Explosive	Dread Panic-stricken Terrified Horrified Petrified Shocked

138

single word to describe a sensation, then it is probably a thought rather than a feeling. Your task here is to learn as much as possible about your emotions. Learn which feelings give you difficulty; which feelings provide you with pleasure, and when and how you cause them to change. I have divided the emotions into five components: THINKING, BEHAVIOR, BODY SENSATION, BODY LANGUAGE, and AROUSAL LEVEL. This is a key to getting a handle on what your feelings "feel like."

ANGER

THINKING: Pessimistic, angry racing thoughts -- "I need my mate to be different; I can't stand it; It shouldn't be this way; I want to fight or run."

BODY LANGUAGE: Waving fists or finger, quick and abrupt movements

BEHAVIOR: Out of control, overly-loud, very assertive and confrontive

BODY SENSATION: Nausea, heart pounding, muscle tension, high energy, fearful

AROUSAL LEVEL: High

JOY

THINKING: Happy, contented thoughts, positive outlook -- "Isn't it a wonderful day, I'm having so much fun."

BODY LANGUAGE: Open hand, welcoming arm gestures, good eye contact, standing tall and erect

BEHAVIOR: Light, uplifting movements, and graceful movements, talkative, engaging others, smiling

BODY SENSATION: Energetic, tingling all over, at ease

AROUSAL LEVEL: Medium

DEPRESSION

THINKING: Hopeless, helpless, pessimistic, doom and gloom -- "I will never be able to find another job; Life will never be the same; Life is meaningless."

BODY LANGUAGE: Head down, poor eye contact, hands and arms close to body

BEHAVIOR: Slow, isolative, non-talkative, withdrawn

BODY SENSATION: Weighty, heavy feeling, no energy

AROUSAL LEVEL: Low

SADNESS

THINKING: Despairing, hopeless, discouraged, unhappy -- "I'm going to miss him so much; It feels so lonely and quiet without him at home; I remember him sitting in that chair smiling at me."

BODY LANGUAGE: Shoulders slumped, frown, teary-eyed

BEHAVIOR: Slow, lethargic, crying

BODY SENSATION: Empty, feels as if something is missing

AROUSAL LEVEL: Moderately low

LONELINESS

THINKING: Sad, bored, hopeless -- "I have nothing to do this weekend; No one ever calls me anymore; The house seems so big and empty."

BODY LANGUAGE: Pulled back, perhaps curled up in a ball

BEHAVIOR: Slow, non-assertive, withdrawn

BODY SENSATION: Empty, numb

AROUSAL LEVEL: Medium-low

BOREDOM

THINKING: Angry, anxious, confused, hostile -- "There is nothing to do; I never seem to have any fun; Life is such a drag."

BODY LANGUAGE: Arms crossed, head down, droopy facial expression

BEHAVIOR: Inactive or near movement without detection, glum, sluggish

BODY SENSATION: Nervous, uncomfortable, agitated, expectant

AROUSAL LEVEL: Medium

FEAR

THINKING: Helpless, worried, panic, can't think clearly -- "I'm so scared; I'm afraid someone will sneak into the house at night and hurt me; I'm sure that this airplane is going to crash and I'll die!"

BODY LANGUAGE: Fists clenched or ready to clench quickly, arms in a protective position, eyes wide open, fast breathing

BEHAVIOR: Defensive, running, pacing, watching, tense, waiting, calculating

BODY SENSATION: Nausea, bad taste in mouth, dread, heart pounding, tense muscles, digestion stopped

AROUSAL LEVEL: High

It is important to realize that feelings are not necessarily realities. Many of the emotions that we experience are merely sensations triggered by both internal and external stimuli, and the four corners of the Pyramid. Some of these are actually phobias, originating years ago as a result of various factors. It is sort of like a cat who hears the can opener and licks his chops, expecting food to be on the way. As with the cat's anticipation, many of our responses occur automatically. I also realize many of these feelings, whether real or imagined, are quite uncomfortable; but the longer you can stay with them, the stronger you will become and the more resistant you will be to relapse. You are building emotional muscle, just as was related to you in the cold swimming pool example given earlier.

One of the foundations of breaking an unhealthy habit and gaining control over your life is learning to be able to tolerate less than optimal emotions. It is important that you learn to "sit with" these emotions; by doing so, you build emotional strength or "emotional muscle."

Every time that you experience a feeling or emotion that you do not like and you don't take a "short-cut" by using your unhealthy habit, you have learned to take control a little more. The more times that you do this, the stronger you become. By using your emotional muscle, you can overcome any stumbling blocks such as unhealthy thoughts, environment, biochemistry, or past behaviors. You are in control by acting in harmony with what is in your best interest. You CAN resist uncomfortable impulses. The more you expose yourself to these uncomfortable feelings, and the more you resist them, the stronger you become. In developing emotional muscle, and by having emotional muscle pre-developed before you need to draw on it will enable you to truly be in control of your life.

Again, let me emphasize that these feelings are more powerful when they remain vague and unidentified. That is why you must be in touch with yourself and know yourself. We are in the process of putting you back in touch with your feelings, and therefore, in charge of your life.

Remember: "Skill Yourself, Don't Kill Yourself!"

Building Emotional Muscle

TAKE CONTROL NOW!

CHAPTER 4   SECRETS FOR SUCCESS

PART 3   CHANGING THINKING -- OVERCOMING "STINKING THINKING"

"I think, therefore I am." (Rene Descartes, 1637)

A concept first put forth in about 100 AD is perhaps the oldest psychological model in history. It proposes that the way we feel is based primarily on how we think. Epictetus said, "Men are disturbed not by things, but by the views which they take of them." Even cavemen, without realizing it, searched for meaning and explanations which would soothe and buffer them against fears of the unknown and the dread of death.

Besides being aware of our own mortality, man differs from other creatures in that we are able to think about thinking. Animals, unable to alter their thinking or to separate themselves from it, are unable to make intentional changes in their lives.

Successful people, if asked about their thinking, would probably say that life is basically good. Even when troubled, such individuals view the world in moderate, non-catastrophic terms. Their cups are half-full, rather than half-empty. Their optimism prevails over pessimism.

Our thinking directly and indirectly affects how we feel about the world in general, how we feel about ourselves and consequently how we act in society. Although we may not reveal our innermost thoughts to other people, our views can often be surmised through our actions, facial expressions and body language. It is important to distinguish between our conscious and unconscious thoughts because both have profound influence on all aspects of our life.

In therapy, we often find that most people who are unhappy are subject to thoughts of dread, fear, disgust, and self-loathing. Needless to say, such thinking has a huge bearing on self-esteem and social interactions.

Today, most contemporary schools of thought essentially concur with the idea that: "If I can change what this person thinks about himself and the world around him, then I have been of help." Whether therapy involves long-term, in-depth analysis or the short-term cognitive-behavioral strategies, methodologies are used to try to identify a client's thought processes in hopes of changing both feelings and behavior.

As we have discussed, the goal here is to teach you how to gain control over your bad habits by changing your thinking -- which changes your behavior -- which alters biochemistry -- which changes feelings -- and so on. Of all the corners of the Pyramid, this is probably the best place to begin. For if we are still in agreement that emotional control is essential in extricating ourselves from destructive behaviors, then learning the principles of how to change thinking should give us the confidence of a new and powerful, ever present tool to control more of our needs.

The prime purpose here is to help you develop a new philosophy about the powers of thought, which will start a positive chain reaction. This positive snowball is the beginning of Pyramid Power.

For ease of discussion, I have chosen the model of Rational-Emotive Therapy (recently renamed Rational-Emotive Behavior Therapy) as developed by Albert Ellis, Ph.D., to explain the basic premises of the powers of thought. There are many other good models, but they all work basically the same way.

In Rational-Emotive Therapy, the basic elements are called the ABC's of RET -- in actuality, it is the ABCDE's of RET (as follows):

A = Activating Events

B = Beliefs

C = Consequences

D = Disputing

E = Effects

Typically in our society, we are taught that A (Activating Event) directly causes a C (Consequence). For example, we may say, "My girlfriend broke up with me (A) so I went out and got drunk!" (C) or "The reason I'm so happy (C) is that I won some money in the lottery!" (A).

However, in RET, as well as other thought challenging methods, we are taught that it is our Beliefs (B) about the Activating Event (A) that causes the Consequential feelings or actions (C). So, according to this concept, it is your belief about your girlfriend leaving that causes anger or depression, and it is not the lottery prize itself that makes you happy, but rather your thoughts and beliefs about money and winning.

In RET, (A) does not cause (C), but rather our BELIEFS about (A) result in (C). It is not your girlfriend leaving that actually causes you to drink, but rather your BELIEF that "I'm never going to find another relationship," and/or "This proves how unattractive I am," and/or "I can't stand this feeling of being alone and rejected and the only way I can handle it is to get drunk." As you can see, all of these thoughts provoke negative feelings and destructive behavior.

The (D) Disputing and E (Effects) take place when we go back and examine our beliefs. At (D), we try to vigorously dispute the irrational beliefs in (B). The truth is: You will find another girlfriend, you won't die if you are alone, and you are not worthless or unattractive just because a particular relationship has ended. Even though it's rough at the moment, you can live through those uncomfortable feelings and grabbing a drink is far from the only thing you can do to feel better.

When you realize and truly accept that many of the things you have been telling yourself are irrational, illogical, false, exaggerated, over-generalized, or at the very least, melodramatic, you can then begin to cultivate more reality-based thoughts. We have all had the experience when our feelings about a particular person have changed drastically after possessing new information. This concept is the foundation of all thought-changing techniques.

Now, let's look at an example where an Activating Event (A) is a feeling, perhaps boredom. The consequence of boredom is often smoking, drinking, or eating. But, the feeling of boredom doesn't cause this behavior. Rather, it is caused by your Belief (B) that "I can't tolerate boredom." or "This feeling is unbearable," or most commonly, "I've got to get rid of this feeling and the only way I can do it is through my habit."

At times, we have a legitimate reason to feel angry or sad or lonely or depressed or bored. But, if you feel very low much of the time and are frequently engaging in unhealthy and destructive behaviors, then chances are that your beliefs are in some way out of perspective -- either distorted, illogical or exaggerated. In order to regain emotional control, you need to stop what you are doing and identify and challenge the errors of your thinking.

If you can learn to apply RET or simply alter your beliefs through affirmations, you will have acquired a powerful emotion-changing tool. This is a tool that will never cost you any money, make you fat, or destroy your health or your mind. If you have been using "Elixirs" to soothe your loneliness or quiet your boredom, you can now -- through new perceptions -- achieve the same effect or result another way. When you do it, it will be much easier to give up those short-cut solutions. Now you will never 'run out' of a fix, because your fix is your belief system. With it, you will enjoy a powerful and positive sense of mastery over your moods, actions and life.

All of this will not happen overnight. The beliefs you have are deeply ingrained. These creations of unrealistic thought processes, such as the idea that "we'll always be fat or unlovable," cause us to act accordingly like a self-fulfilling prophecy. Only by persistently searching our minds and asking "What am I telling myself?" -- and then combatting those self-fulfilling prophecies can we overcome them. Our belief system has phenomenal power over us -- but it is changeable. You can change it!

An example of this is how easily we can change our beliefs about others. Sometimes, we particularly like or dislike someone; then we receive new information. Perhaps we discover that a co-worker whom we thought to be aloof and a snob has a terminally ill child. Perhaps we learn that a 'heart-of-gold' neighbor is actually a thief in the department store where she works. With that kind of powerful new input, we are sure to revise our opinions -- and consequently, our feelings and behavior toward them change quite rapidly. Although altering our beliefs about ourselves is more complicated, you will eventually encounter the magic of change as you start to increase your control.

What we have covered here is only an introduction to RET, and these techniques warrant much more study and exploration. In your on-going struggle to identify those thoughts that lead to feelings and actions, be on the look-out for internal dialogues involving words such as 'have to' or 'must' or 'should.' Also, pay attention to catastrophic expectations and self-defeating thoughts. You might not even be aware of such internal dialogues -- but if you are feeling traumatized or depressed over some recent event, I can assure you that you have probably been feeding yourself some very exaggerated, catastrophic and self-damning thoughts. Now is the time to take control and begin to challenge all negative and irrational thinking. Take a look again at the Power Pyramid, and try to come up with some of your own creative ideas for coping with distressing emotions. The following is a listing of some of the most popular, time-tested methods of changing thinking and therefore coping.

- Yoga
- Meditation
- Positive Affirmations
- Hypnosis
- Spirituality
- Books
- Television
- Films
- Theatre
- Videos
- Fantasy

- Singing/Whistling

- Seminars & Workshops

- Focused Conversations, in a group or one to one

- Visualization Techniques

- Volunteer Work

- Motivational Tapes

- Journal Writing/Diary

- Laughter

- Doing something nice for someone

- Thought stopping (Screaming "STOP" in your mind when your thinking becomes negative.)

- Psychotherapy -- most all current approaches incorporate the idea that if old thinking patterns can be seen and understood by mature rationale, even childhood traumas can become less painful.

- Addictive Voice Recognition

ULTIMATE THOUGHTS IN FREEING YOURSELF FROM UNHEALTHY HABITS

No discussion on thought-changing as a tool for combatting unhealthy habits would be complete without a few more comments. It must be recognized that within every one of us there are thousands of thoughts that are 'important to' and 'supportive of' your habit. It is therefore helpful to regard these thoughts as one more associated process that must be changed, because these often circular, self-damning, hopeless concepts are an unhealthy habit in themselves. As such, they must be vigorously assailed if you are to transcend into a much happier lifestyle. If you think you can end a particular habit without changing your related thinking -- you are wrong -- for you will always be 'white-knuckling' it and on the verge of relapse.

I would like to offer some thoughts on "thinking styles." In my clinical experience, I have found that there are two basic styles which undermine taking control and changing, more than anything else. They can be summarized this way: "I can't stand feeling uncomfortable." and "It's too hard!" As you can see, these attitudes are similar in their refusal to tolerate discomfort. There are no short-cuts --"JUST DO IT!" Internal action equals internal reaction. DOING builds self confidence. AVOIDANCE lowers self-esteem. The power of the relationship between doing and self-confidence is monumental. Break down new tasks into small increments. Building new behavior traits can be done in small, easily attainable steps. Be comfortable in your body and don't respond to guilt or compulsions. Don't numb out, just take one step at time. Expect some anxiety, discomfort and failure when making changes in your behavior. Remember -- no pain, no gain.

RELAPSE AND THINKING

Let's do another ABC. This example I find more common than almost any problem in taking control of people's unhealthy habits.

A (Activating Event) Used my "Elixir" (bad habit) last night

B (Consequence) Depressed, hopeless and continued to use my "Elixir" (bad habit)

So, what do you imagine is the belief that might cause the above Activating Event to cause you to relapse? Here are some potential suggested thoughts:

B (Beliefs)

1.   See, I can't do this!

2.   This book doesn't work.

151

3.   I will never be able to stop, it's just too hard.

4.   This proves that I'm weak.

5.   Other people are smarter that I am because I am the only one who relapses!

6.   My friends and family will be very angry and I can't face them!

7.   I must not be doing something right because I relapsed.

8.   I'm no good and this proves it.

9.   It should be easier!

This is just a short list of the possible beliefs that you might tell yourself about a relapse.

Here are some rational, logical thoughts on what you might tell yourself at D (Disputing) that will lead to a better E (Effect):

1.   Statistics prove that most people relapse at some point during their recovery from unhealthy habits. In fact, relapse is a wonderful time to learn what you need to do differently, and it helps break through the denial of what large energies are needed to chang an unhealthy habit. Also, just because you have slipped, you don't need to give yourself an excuse to slip again. Slips do not need to escalate into full-blow use again unless you want them to.

2.   Just because I have a relapse, it doesn't prove anything. It doesn't mean that you can't do it or the book, the support group, the therapy doesn't work -- or that it will be too hard. All it means is that it is harder than you thought. So, pick yourself-up and dig yo heels in deeper. Relapse also doesn't mean that you have to start over -- you have learned a lot about yourself, just build on it.

3.   Just because I had a relapse, doesn't mean anything about my self-worth. Habits are very hard to break, but it doesn't mean that I am bad or that I am weak.

4.   My friends' and families' feelings have nothing to do with my relapse. They don't really understand my unique situation, even if they have broken a bad habit themselves. If they are angry, so what! That's their problem, isn't it?

5.   Who said that it should be easier? Why should it be easier? It is as hard as it is -- no less, no more. If it were really easy, people wouldn't write books about it and there wouldn't be such a large industry in providing recovery treatment. It is very hard, but it isn't too hard!!

6.   Relapse is normal, therefore I am normal. Similarly, if I don't challenge those irrational beliefs (B), my self-esteem will suffer. On the other hand, if I learn to dispute and challenge those beliefs, as in (D), I will feel better and have a more honest view of my self-esteem and worth.

"DO I NEED TO BE RELIGIOUS?"

[Dr. Kern's personal comments]

There is significant controversy over the role of religion, being part of a Higher Power, in overcoming unhealthy habits. Basically, religious concepts are just one way of changing beliefs so that we can respond differently with a new perspective. Religion, therefore, can be conceptualized under the heading, "Changing Thinking to Change Feelings and Behavior." It can be a very useful tool in long-term recovery. Our purpose here isn't to promote a particular way of changing thinking, but rather to explore many different methods.

The ancient Egyptians believed in life after death, because their lives were often filled with toil and suffering. Their belief in Nirvana offered them hope, which translates into the thought: "Things won't always be this way."

Many people turn to unhealthy habits because their concept of life is hopeless -- a vacuum of emptiness and despair. "Why am I here?" - "Why Should I bother?" - "Why not go for the quick-fix?" This mind-set is particularly relevant in the lower socioeconomic strata, and is grimly evidenced in the mentality of today's young gang members. "Why not shoot the guy who killed my homeboy?" - "I'll be dead in a couple of years anyway." In the face of hopelessness, there is little reason to avoid unhealthy habits, no compelling reason to behave differently.

Religion, however, is an important force which does act to motivate people to change their behavior. That is why I want to encourage its use as one method of changing. I feel that it is important to legitimatize it as a valid method, one viable way of finding inner peace. It is one more weapon in your toolkit of strategies to create a good feeling inside, which will lessen your need for unhealthy habits.

A question often asked is, "Do I have the right religion?" Of course, no one can answer that but you. Whatever faith, group of people, or philosophy that makes sense to you, bolsters you, and gives you hope is what you should pursue.

Similarly, the concept of spirituality needs to be mentioned within this context. Because spirituality means so many different things to different people, I am going to avoid any strict definitions. If you consider yourself spiritual or find spiritual concepts helpful, I want to strongly encourage you in that direction. If through your own spiritual explorations you find inner peace, comfort, or connections, you should by all means encourage and develop this resource to its maximum potential.

On the other hand, if religion and spirituality are not concepts that you feel comfortable with, you needn't feel that your chances for recovery from your habits have been compromised. I personally know hundreds of individuals, and have read about thousands of others, who have conquered their bad habits without these concepts playing any role. The goal of this book is to encourage and direct you toward finding your own path to the controls of life and recovery from your unhealthy habits.

There is no right way, but rather as many ways as there are people. Any modality that facilitates and clarifies your thinking will alter your biochemistry, and instill a feeling of inner peace.

If escapist entertainment seems to serve that purpose for you, don't concern yourself with political or artistic correctness. Art films and classics are fine if you really enjoy them, but if action hero films or tabloids help change your mood or mind-set then don't hesitate to use them.

With all that said, I do believe that we Humans need a sort of belief system that answers the question: "What is the meaning or purpose of life?" Without such a foundation, we are more apt to suffer from "lack of direction" and unexplained anxiety. While a comprehensive discussion of this topic is beyond the scope of this book, I want to encourage each of you to explore and find an answer to this question that is right for you.

At the very root of this question is our denial of the "fear of death." We search for meaning or purpose to rationalize our existence and our mortality. Whatever you believe does not alter the fact that none of us get off this planet alive. All you can do is to choose a meaning that personally works for you, be it religion, an activity or a philosophy -- and keep moving onward.

CHAPTER 5 DEVELOPING YOUR NEW HEALTHY HABITS--FOCUSING ON YOU

PART 1 USING YOUR UNIQUE FACTOR

> "Sometimes I hear my name
>
> come up the stairs and walk
>
> through noises in the hall;
>
> but sounds all seem the same
>
> in here, alone at night. . .
>
> I never answer back
>
> to sounds that seem the same
>
> as those that make my name;
>
> For noises in the hall
>
> are not MY name at all!"

This quote from Horace Gregory's poem, "A Boy of Twenty," is how you may feel from time to time at this point. You have been developing the 'mental muscle' to combat your old unhealthy habits and replace them with new healthy habits. However, sometimes a night or when you are under stress, you think you can hear your old unhealthy habit "calling out your name through the noise," beckoning and tempting you, like a siren, to slip backward into the quicksand of the "Short-Cut Life" and into the welcoming arms of your old unhealthy behavior.

You each have a "Unique Factor," something that makes you an individual who is totally different from anyone else. This Unique Factor is free to 'shine through' and become evident to everyone, if it has not been masked by one or more unhealthy habits. When you practice unhealthy habits, even if you practice them in total secrecy, they have such a dynamic negative effect on your behavior that you, in essence, become the unhealthy habit. It is always on your mind, subtly controlling your thoughts and actions. So, the face that you present to the public isn't the 'real you.' Instead, it is you being influenced by your unhealthy habits in a most influential way. Once the unhealthy behavior has been replaced with healthy habits, the underlying Unique Factor, which is the 'real you,' is free to shine through. Suddenly, the people that you associate with and meet are introduced to a one-of-a-kind person whom they like and remember. They no longer see a person with a limited personality. They see a multi-dimensional person, not just a gray lump that they can easily forget or pass by.

According to one of the world's foremost psychiatrists, Dr. William C. Menninger, there are seven keys of emotional maturity that should help unlock your Unique Factor. The following pages are quotes and paraphrases of Dr. Menninger's philosophies and work, and are consistent with my beliefs and views about changing your unhealthy habits.

The first of Dr. Menninger's keys is "Face Reality. . . ." Reality means the world that we live in, with all the hostility that surrounds us. Selfishness, suspicion, lack of understanding, pursuit by witch-hunters, dishonesty, disappointment, loss and many, many more attitudes and experiences makes reality and life very difficult at times.

". . . If we are reasonably mature, we can play the cards that are dealt to us in life, keeping in mind that we have much to say about these cards, and even quite a little about the game to which we sit down.

"If we are healthy, it means that we have learned how to accept frustration with a fair degree of grace in order to gain something we want in the future. Unfortunately, there are people who continue the childhood practice of demanding, 'I want what I want when I want it, and something will pop if I don't get it.'

"They have never learned to accept what reality is -- namely that if something is worth having, it requires effort, saving and planning.

"Being able to deal constructively with reality implies that we have developed other intangible qualities that make us feel secure enough to tolerate delay in gaining satisfaction.

"There are two types of security. One is the peace of mind which comes from an inner reservoir of strength, so that when the going gets rough, we don't get jittery, jumpy, and upset. This serenity allows us to stand some pretty high waves. Then, there is the necessity for external security. In this, our experience can vary so widely--from a very secure home, to existence in a foxhole. Insecurity may be brought on by family situations, or by relations with other people.

". . . Emotional maturity implies the refusal, inappropriately, to take flight or to fight when faced with difficult reality. It is easy to run when the blows of reality fall. We find many ways of doing just that. If we wish, we can go to sleep and momentarily escape our thoughts. Sometimes, we become ill in order to run away.

"We can watch other people use innumerable ways to avoid or to fight reality. Most often, fighting a situation destroys rather then improves the situation.

"Rarely, if ever, does becoming angry help. We have learned the hard way that worldwide combat as well as personal fighting brings destruction.

"As mature individuals, we must devise ways of facing reality by neither taking flight or fighting, but by making constructive compromises.

"Key number two is 'Adapt To Change.' Life is a continuing series of changes. An individual is a constantly changing person. Changes in ourselves may or may not correspond to changes in the environment in which we live. The most noticeable feature of our present way of life is the almost unbelievable number of changes, sometimes from hour to hour, in the way we live which are the result of the things with which we work, the gadgets that surround us, the different areas in which we function.

"Our present era is one of such rapid change that many of us feel great concern as to whether the destructive power of man can be.controlled.

". . . Daily, each of us is confronted with new experiences and opportunities which require adaption and growth -- on the job, as a parent, or as a citizen.

". . . Parents of today cannot use the same rules as their mothers and fathers. Failure to grow causes problems. We recognize 'that other person' who is so rigid in their thinking and actions that they cannot change at all. We are annoyed that he cannot adapt himself to conform to the new rules, and we describe him as being stubborn.

"There is also the example of the adult who continues to use the same kind of device he used to solve childhood problems. They rely upon the same kind of explanations and alibis. It is in our early and formative years that we develop our basic pattern of response which becomes modified if we mature, or remains the same if we do not mature.

". . . If we are to be mature, we must have resiliency, no matter what our age, to adjust, to adapt, to change.

"The third key is 'Control Anxieties.' This can be described as having relative freedom from symptoms that are produced by tensions and anxieties. Remember, I said RELATIVE freedom. Things happen in the lives of all of us . . . that have affected our

159

personalities. Early life experiences have warped some individuals to a considerable degree; on others they have set such limits on their emotional maturity that what was an adequate response at age six is still used at age forty six. But, now it is no longer appropriate. However, in most of us, these early experiences have established basic patterns which have been modified later.

"When there is a conflict between reality and what we are and do, tension and anxiety may be felt.

"We may express this tension and anxiety by unreasonableness, illogical thinking, irrational behavior, or in physical symptoms such as headaches or stomach pains. In psychiatric terminology, these are called 'neurotic evasions.'

"We have friends who are far too aggressive, so aggressive that it is difficult to be around them. . . . They must try to keep the center stage, they are so conceited [headstrong] that it is difficult to listen to them.

"There are also those among us that are too passive, so passive that they do not do anything, and incidentally and paradoxically, they are aggressive in their passivity. They are the hangers-on. Something happened in their early childhoods that left them feeling comfortable only when holding onto someone's apron strings far and beyond the time they should have reached out for independence.

"There are also people who are very shy and therefore lonesome. They would like to be in the swim [of things], but they don't quite know how to manage it.

"Perhaps they received severe psychological injuries from running into social or emotional buzz saws which made them fear becoming hurt [or embarrassed] again.

". . . Many of us feel inadequate too much of the time, and at times we all do [experience feelings of inadequacy]. [This is a normal human experience, as we cannot be 100% proficient in everything that challenges us.]

"It is the individual who never feel inadequate for whom I really feel sorry. But, there are [people in the society] described as feeling inferior; they never have the right clothes; they can't "keep up with the Jones;" They compare themselves unfavorably to others and feel miserable about it. This is clearly self-punishment which stems from a personality problem of early life.

"Quite apart from these, in order to get along with other people, all of us learn to use psychological devices that are termed 'defense mechanisms' -- escapes.

"One of the most used defense mechanisms is 'rationalization,' a simple definition of which is: 'Something of which I am quite sure and which justifies my belief in it and my right to argue about it' -- even though the person doing the rationalization is actually in error.

"Rationalization enables one to resist a difference of opinion because he/she is confident about his rationalized beliefs. The attitude is: 'Don't try to convince me with the facts because my mind is already made up.'

". . . Another way to avoid problems is to blame others for our own faults. This is called 'projection.' An example would be: 'It isn't my fault that we lost the game, it is Jeff's fault for fumbling the ball.' Whatever is wrong is the other person's responsibility.

". . . We would be wiser, and we would see ourselves and the state of our mental health -- the degree of our emotional maturity -- more clearly if we could recognize our use of these various devices for what they are.

". . . There are some people who enjoy their symptoms of tension and anxiety [headaches, stomach problems, irregular heart beats, etc.] while others think they can do nothing about them until they understand their cause. However, you don't have to know the cause of a fire to start putting it out. . . . This simple principle also applies in the reduction and elimination of our tensions [and anxieties]. Look for the source and start putting out the flames.

"The fourth key is 'Give of Yourself.' Develop the capacity to find more satisfaction in giving than in receiving. We come into this world 100% on the receiving end of the line -- with everything coming our way. Gradually, the process reverses itself. From the point of view of mental health, the mature adult is most often on the giving end; however, no one should give up ALL gratification from receiving, for others also, want to give.

"In fact, much giving results in receiving appreciation. We give love and enjoy receiving it in return. Obviously, if one gives only to be rewarded or as a way of demanding appreciation, his motive is not a healthy one.

"The less mature person asks, 'What has that to do with me?' 'What do I get out of it?'

"In contrast, the more mature person's questions are: 'What has that to do with us?' -- 'What can we contribute?' -- 'What can we put into it?'

"There is also a relationship between one's capacity to give and what he receives. All of us have the need to depend on someone else. We 'need' other meaningful people in our lives or we miss much life has to offer. . . . We need to have refueling stations, no matter how autonomous we think we are -- quiet times, vacations, good friends, etc. Receiving and renewing make it possible to become . . . 'a real person.'

"... For the best mental health, and emotional maturity, the individual should have a cause, a mission, an aim in life that is constructive and that is so big he has to keep working on it.

"Good and interesting causes with constructive opportunities exist in every community [that fit into our own individual personality structures, talents, and interests. Building a new, healthy life for yourself that uses your talents and expertise is one of the best vitamin pills that you can take for emotional maturity, strength, and sound mental health.]

"Key number five is 'Consider Others.' . . . If we look superficially at our current social order, we see much evidence of failures of people to get along with each other -- the number of broken homes, the discharge rate in business and industry of which a large percent is due to social, not technical, incompetence.

"[Some] people in our midst cannot play the game by the rules on which the rest of us agree. They are poor sports, delinquents, and criminals.

"Others delight in scapegoating and witch hunting. Bickering and sniping are engaged in between all kinds of groups: social, racial, economic, political, and religious.

"The capacity of getting along with each other depends on various factors in our individual personalities. Going back to a personality trait that has already been mentioned: [People] cannot get along harmoniously with other people unless [they] are willing to GIVE [OF THEMSELVES]. [We can generalize by saying that,] the person who gives most probably gets along best, not because other people bleed him, but because he finds satisfaction in working with them. This requires the ability to identify with others, to try to understand them even when they are difficult.

163

"One does not necessarily have to agree with someone else, at least entirely, or even approve of certain actions in order to respect him.

"Another measure of emotional maturity is whether you are able to form a permanent loyalty, not merely to those who are personally advantageous to our position, but to those who are part of our team at the workplace or in our social environment.

". . . If we can relate comfortably to other people, this is mutually helpful and stimulating. In contrast, is the person who seems to get enjoyment out of making other people unhappy by being mean, making excessive demands, by restrictive or punitive attitudes or by being neglectful.

". . . The good employer [or manager], who in a literal sense is a figurative father figure, is considerate of his employees, the teacher of his pupils. [He is effective because he tries to understand human behavior instead of alienating it and hiding behind a code of rigid rules or conduct.]

"There are personality traits or characteristics which, with all our marvelous development in the field of psychology and personality testing, we have not found a way to test and measure -- some of the most important traits that we know the mature person has. They develop from the experience of growing, learning, adapting, and adopting.

"Perhaps one of the most important of these personality traits is sincerity.

"We can quickly sense whether a person is sincere or insincere [by his mannerisms, tone of voice, and actions.]

"How do we recognize or measure integrity -- that combination of honesty, fairness, dependability, and willingness to assume responsibility?

"How do we learn to accept criticism, from which we should lean and profit without throwing up the walls of our defense mechanisms and dismiss the criticism without leaning and maturing from it?

"How do we learn to win modestly and to lose graciously?

"All of these are facets of our capacity to relate to other people. . . . We can each learn to look at ourselves objectively enough to see where we need to improve. [If we act on accomplishing those improvements, then we have taken a giant step toward emotional maturity.]

"The sixth key is 'Curb Hostility.' . . . You must have the capacity to subliminate, to direct your instinctive hostile energy into creative and constructive outlets. We all possess constructive and destructive drives. It is our emotions that get us into trouble -- our destructive, aggressive impulses. [It seems that] most of the time we do not even recognize these emotions, they are so successfully hidden from our conscious stream of thinking.

"The recognition of our own aggressive acts, our own aggressive impulses, is basic to channeling them into constructive channels which is so important if we are able to be emotionally mature and mentally healthy.

"At times, we turn this hostility onto ourselves. Unreasonable feelings of guilt, inferiority, the guilt that tortures -- for which there is no known cause -- are examples of feelings that can paralyze us and prevent our doing something worthwhile. All of us have a certain degree of self-defeatism [but it is this uncontrolled feeling which is unhealthy and destructive.]

". . . The pettiness, the hostilities, and the aggressions are also turned on society in general by those who lack social responsibility. Such a prevalent attitude among many individuals of 'Me first!' is not healthy for the community or for the individual. Paternalism increases as more people expect some sort of handout. It manifests itself as a matter of pride for those who brag about how much they get away with. Hostility is also expressed by cheating and stinginess.

"Hate can be subliminated, it can be directed into constructive outlets. It is the mature person who finds ways to do this, in the home, the work place, and the community by engaging in activities [that give his life a new purpose and a new center of attraction that is rewarding and fulfilling.]

"The seventh and final key is 'Learn to Love.' Finally, the seventh criterion, and the most important, is having the capacity to love. By 'love,' I refer to a broad usage of the word -- caring. How do we learn to care? As infants, if we were fortunate, we had parents that expressed their love by looking after us, [and tenderly touching us.] . . . We learned to love in return by developing an interdependence in our initial family.

"Next, we learned to like and enjoy being with other people, to give affection, and to have an interest in those outside the family. . . . The ideal from which true self-happiness can come is the hope that all of us might continue and extend our caring beyond the family, to our community, to our state, to our nation, and to a very small world.

"There aren't enough people who have developed the capacity to care and have the recognition that killing people, [being self-centered, hurting people, and being indifferent] will not solve problems -- [it only adds to the problems.] . . . [Caring and] love [are] the only neutralizing agents for hate.

". . . The world is filled with hate. Hate is like an acid that eats away at all other feeling and emotions. Hate begins in the minds of men -- yours and mine. If we care enough, we must see this hate [for the primitive animal passion that it is] and hopefully help more people [learn by our example how to care and] love more until all hate is neutralized."

These seven keys as quoted and paraphrased from works by Dr. Menninger can help you focus on your Unique Factor and aid you in building a new and fulfilling life for yourself that excludes your unhealthy habits. It is work to build healthy new behavior, but by building new structures, and learning how to work the Pyramid, you can do it.

Remember: "Skill Yourself, Don't Kill Yourself."

CHAPTER 5 DEVELOPING YOUR NEW HEALTHY HABITS--FOCUSING ON YOU

PART 2 CHANGING BEHAVIOR

The following is a general discussion, not a precise blueprint that outlines making change.

Over the years in working with my clients, when someone expresses feelings of being disliked or unlovable, I suggest that he/she try just one new behavior. Perhaps it is standing up to a parent or telling a spouse about some issue that has been an aggravation. Any action at all will work, as long as it is something new. As often as I have done this, I never cease to be amazed when a client returns with a remarkable new sense of 'self.' For one single ordinary act of assertiveness automatically causes a change in self-perception, and therefore, a new more positive feeling.

New behavior also plays a central role in giving up unhealthy habits. That doesn't just include actions involving the unhealthy habit itself. Altering additional behaviors is important in order to change over-all thinking and feeling patterns, for ultimately these new feelings are what will lessen your needs.

I remember one client, a successful businessman in his forties, who had long been addicted to stress and had become a workaholic. In spite of all he provided for his family -- an elegant home, status, luxury cars, charge accounts, etc. -- his wife of twenty years was threatening to leave him. "Our children will be going to college," Steve explained, "and I guess she feels like there's no use sticking around if I'm never there. She wants more of a relationship and I don't know how to do that anymore."

Somewhere along the line, years earlier when his wife had been busy juggling children and a real estate career, Steve had felt unloved and unimportant. He responded by stepping up his own business and became dependent on stress and work. The fast-track pace worked for a while, until Steve's wife began to realize she needed more out of life than just 'things.' She demanded a change in their marriage or else!

Steve was both hurt and angry. Although he realized the validity of his wife's ultimatum, he didn't have any idea about how to change his lifestyle and maintain his self-esteem. "If I slow down, I'm afraid I'll lose it all. I don't know how to be different any more. At work, I get a great deal of respect and compliments, and I feel good. When I come home, all I hear are complaints, and then I start feeling lousy -- and that makes me want to lock myself up with my computer for the rest of the night so I can focus on my business and shut everything else out. I created this business -- I am it and it is me. I know what it is. I'm good at it and it protects me."

I asked Steve to begin with the first step of taking Sunday's off and planning activities with his wife. I told Steve to "Pretend that she is a client, and plan lots of activities and do them whether you like them or not." He shook his head and walked out of my office unconvinced.

He returned the next week in a different mood. "I can't believe it," Steve explained. "I was really mad at first, I felt like why should I cater to my wife when she's threatening to leave me! By the end of the day which had been full of fun activities, we had dinner at that new French restaurant in the city and I just started to feel different. I mean she wouldn't be giving this ultimatum if all she wanted was my money!"

By changing just one small behavior you will find that proceeding to the next step will be easier for you. It is imperative to change your actions, for they impact on your unhealthy habits in dozens of subtle ways. Only by becoming more active and trying new things will you start to learn a new set of coping strategies that will help you get to the root of the problem.

Every unhealthy habit is made up of thousands of little behaviors which on the surface may seem unrelated. That is why it is so crucial to realize the importance of changing patterns of passivity, thrill-seeking, isolation or boredom, and avoidance with new activities.

There are several ways to change behavior once you understand the dynamics. For example, if you have been sedating your feelings of boredom or nervousness through isolation or with excessive television or drugs, you must now develop alternative ways of regulating those moods. Perhaps you will start by breaking up the time that you watch television with a walk around the block every half hour; or just take the batteries out of the remote control and it will force you to move out of your chair, and thereby change your behavior. If you are nervous, try a hot tub, a steamy shower, soft music, or buy yourself a pet. You must make a start, then everything after that initial start will be easier for you.

If boredom is your downfall, work on increasing your energy level. Join a sports club, or a gym. Try your skill at playing video games, or listen to your favorite music. As long as a new activity appeals to you, it will work as an alternative method for increasing energy. Even though some of your habits seem unrelated to your unhealthy behavior, they are very much a part of your whole behavioral repertoire and need to be adjusted or replaced.

Currently, your unhealthy habit has a major dominance on your life. What you need is a whole menu of selections. The bottom line is this: If you are passive, work hard toward becoming more assertive. If you have always been hyperactive, learn how to slow down. A good change for you might be just learning how to sit quietly when you are in a car with friends, rather than feeling compelled to fill every moment with chatter. Perhaps you need to stop frantically trying to please everyone. Take control, and change what you have been doing! Stretch your behavioral envelope. Whether it is Yoga, martial arts, jogging, or knitting, just force yourself to stretch. Try new activities and make a point of stretching in social situations, in your personal life and in your work.

Remember, when you try something new, you can expect a certain amount of anxiety or discomfort. That is a natural sign -- you know that you are on the 'right track' rather than just 'doing the same old thing in the same old way and getting the same old tired results.' The 'no pain, no gain' principle applies here. If a new activity or behavior doesn't feel uncomfortable at first, it probably means you are not challenging yourself and learning something new and worth doing. Stretching, whether physical, social, or emotional, always causes a little agony at first.

If you are a basically passive natured person, you aren't going to become a 'ball of fire' overnight. If you're a classic type "A" personality (an energetic, 'go-getter'), you're never going to be the most mellow person in the room. You can modify yourself -- you can push toward that middle ground between isolation and social mania. Stretch! Learn how to be in your body comfortably, without responding to guilts and compulsions, without hyperactivity or behaviors that cause you to numb out. You don't need a 180 degree turnabout -- just move -- take one step at a time.

Another important issue in changing your behavior is reflected on the Pyramid Power chart. Specifically, certain behaviors will produce changes in your social environment, a change in your thinking will alter your biochemistry, and ultimately cause a change in your mood

Of all the things you do, perhaps the most important is to begin some kind of exercise program. Physical activity will alter your biochemistry and boost your energy. It will change the way you think about yourself and therefore impact your feelings. It is therapeutic and the effects are remarkable. Not only is exercise beneficial to your heart and lungs, but it improves your immune system, speeds up your metabolism, helps prevent or control the adult onset of diabetes, strengthens bone and muscle and fights depression. In general, it makes you feel good about yourself!

Try something easy at first, such as a short daily walk. The important thing is to find some new activity . . . one you truly enjoy . . . otherwise you will never stick with it. Instead of signing up for a two-year stint at a gym, ask for a short-term plan. You may pay a premium, but at least you will have a chance to find out if it is right for you. If the health club scene doesn't suit you, try something else like nature hikes, ballroom dancing, golf or tennis lessons, jazzercise, aerobics via home video, or bowling. There are many, many options at your disposal today -- just keep trying until you find one that you like. Once you get into a routine, you will find that exercise will become a new and welcome healthy habit and a vitally important ingredient in changing your lifestyle for the better. Remember, this means giving up being a procrastinator, pain avoider, couch potato, etc.

In stabilizing yourself against the merry-go-round of your unhealthy habit, you need to develop AND keep healthy structures (behaviors and thinking) to stay on the right path. It

172

DEVELOPING AND KEEPING HEALTHY STRUCTURES

Use the chart below to list those healthy structures that are vital to your continuing recovery. If there are specific people or activities or thoughts you need to avoid, also list those. Refer to this list regularly to check yourself, and to make sure that you are continuing to stay with important positive structures while avoiding negative structures. Remember, developing all the structures you will need may take a long time and many attempts. Keep trying, add new ones as needed, take control and don't give up!

I NEED TO INTEGRATE THESE POSITIVE STRUCTURES.	Date of 1st attempt	Date of 2nd attempt	Date of next attempt	Date structure stabilized
I AM AVOIDING THESE NEGATIVE STRUCTURES.	Date of 1st attempt	Date of 2nd attempt	Date of next attempt	Date structure stabilized

is easy to develop a new structure when you are motivated, only to drop it once your motivation wanes, and then you start to drift back to your old way of life. Charting your new structures (behaviors and thinking) and checking occasionally to make sure what new structures you need to develop, significantly help keep you on track.

The bottom line is that unless you make behavioral changes, nothing else will change. You can read this book and other self-help manuals, or try to change your thinking as described in previous chapters, or attempt to change your diet, but nothing helps you stick with it as much as seeing your behavior confirm your beliefs. Talk is cheap! You can talk about change all day long, but it is not going to make any difference unless you actually DO the things you think and talk about.

You must put your words into action! It is the only way that this process is going to work. Every time you come up with an excuse, you throw away an opportunity to convince yourself that success is possible.

BUILDING SELF-CONFIDENCE

Closely connected with the section above is the concept of "building of self-confidence." We hear that term bandied around a lot, but self-confidence is nothing more than a belief based on past actions or inactions. If your self-confidence is low, you are going to believe that anything that comes down the road will be too much to handle. You learned this by procrastinating. Perhaps you didn't speak up in class or failed to push hard enough to achieve a goal. Your degree of confidence will increase only when you get out there, take charge, and do it!

Client after client has come into my office and said: "Doctor Kern, I think I could do this if only I were more self-confident." I respond, "You have it backward -- you will only become more self-confident if you do it." The point is there are no short-cuts. You must do that which you have been avoiding, or not only will your habit continue, but you will go on feeling bad about yourself. You can rationalize all you want, but you are aware every time you shy away from something you should be doing. The power of the relationship between 'doing' and self-confidence is monumental. It's a great example of the snowball effect in both directions, positive and negative. Each time you demonstrate through an action that you can do something new, your self-esteem increases. With each step up the confidence ladder, you will find it easier to take on the next hurdle, contributing to still more confidence.

On the other hand, every time that you avoid a difficult task, your self-esteem goes down, making the next time around that much harder. Sometimes, this process is so ingrained that people's lives contract to the point where even the smallest tasks seem overwhelming. There is only one way to go, other than down, and that is up! Stretch your behavioral limits. Push yourself to do things that are uncomfortable, and you will find that not only can you accomplish more than you thought, but you will be laying the foundation for future self-confidence. One of the most important keys is that you break down your tasks into incremental and easily attainable steps. If you set up small steps for yourself, over time you will slowly, but surely, build the confidence to attain even higher goals.

Continuing with this reasoning, and combining it with the concept that certain things are beyond control, there is one skill you must learn if you are to be permanently free from your unhealthy habits.

That one thing is this: "Learn To Sit With Your Emotions!" I realize this is a chapter on changing behavior. In the situation of some distressing emotions, very often the best thing to do with these feelings is NOTHING! Remember, if you do not give in, you are actually changing -- by NOT changing the feeling. The single most important thing to learn is that when an uncomfortable emotion arises, YOU DO NOT NEED TO CHANGE IT!

An example of this is as follows: Remember when you participated in high school or college physical education classes. It seemed that the locker rooms were always poorly ventilated, so when you first walked into them, you would immediately notice a strong smell of shower steam, dirty laundry, disinfectants to clean the floor and toilet facilities, and pungent odors of alcohol, liniment, and other creams and/or ointments used to treat strained muscles. At first, it seemed that this strange brew of odors would take your breath away and you would want to leave the locker room at once. However, the longer you stayed in that atmosphere the less and less you noticed the smell -- until finally, you didn't notice it at all. In essence, you learned to "sit with your emotions" and soon you got used to them and had to do nothing to change them. You learned that your emotions and feelings were not intolerable.

You have been using your unhealthy habit to change your mood when you become uncomfortable or bored. Now, it is very important that you learn that these emotions are not intolerable. The only way you can do this is to demonstrate to yourself that as uncomfortable as it might be, you can stay with your feelings without hitting the "escape button" and turning to your unhealthy habit. This might involve just sitting and letting the feelings exist, or it might mean not running to the refrigerator, or not having another cigarette. Instead, try the following:

- Attempt to distance yourself from the panic associated with the feeling. (Feelings are normal, but people with unhealthy behaviors often attribute abnormal power to them.)

- Take some deep, cleansing breaths.

- Create your own audio tape in which you discuss your feelings and your reactions to them -- then play it often!

- Analyze your thoughts about your emotions, and replace exaggerations and over-dramatizations with clear objective thinking.

- Try to "hover" over an emotion; if you absolutely cannot tolerate it, then use techniques like bursts of fast exercise.

- Try to maintain perspective and your sense of humor, remembering at all times that feelings are only feelings and they will not kill you.

- Soak in a tub of hot water or shower until your body is totally relaxed. (Physical relaxation is a direct and reliable way to soothe up-tight feelings.)

- Treat yourself to a professional massage.

- Call a reliable and trusted friend.

- Play some of your favorite music.

- Write down what you are feeling and the thoughts that result.

- Play a relaxation or meditation audio tape.

- Put your situation into global perspective: Think how lucky you are compared to the millions of people in the world who are victims of war, famine, and disasters.

- Stay grounded in reality; focus on the fact that a particular feeling is just one small part of your being and your life.

- Resolve to push through the discomfort, and end up feeling stronger and better as a result.

- Give yourself some special treat--anything except your unhealthy habit!

There are two final points. First, emotions also work on the principle of adaptation. That means like a cold swimming pool, if you stay in long enough, you will finally get used to it. Secondly, the longer you can stay with that uncomfortable feeling the more self-confidence you will develop along with "emotional muscle." Emotional muscle is nothing more than the ability to tolerate increasing degrees of discomfort. Without developing substantially more emotional muscle than you have now, you will never be able to ride out life's ups and downs. I don't care how wealthy you are or how lucky you seem to be, life is very painful at times and you must learn to tolerate those occasions without returning to your unhealthy habit.

You need to start today by "working out" your emotional muscle until you find that you are a lot stronger than you ever thought possible.

USING THE RIGHT TOOL

I would now like to suggest a framework which helps you select non-destructive distractions and more appropriate arousal regulating activities.

We are all creatures with different arousal styles and our optimal state varies according to the time of day. We need to understand that at times we will want to increase our energy level and at other times, reduce it. Some of you will desire more arousal-increasing activities and others will pursue the opposite. It doesn't matter which type you are, just select the strategy that moves you in your desired direction.

Since we want to stop using unhealthy behavioral habits to accomplish these goals, I have constructed a chart which you can complete as you move along. The chart suggests alternative arousal-increasing and arousal-decreasing activities which you can turn to when you want to change your energy level. Since everyone is different, it allows you to select those methods that best fit your personality and lifestyle. It is imperative that you have several different activities readily available when you need them. You will find none of these different activities work as quickly or effectively as your unhealthy habit; therefore, it is important to start integrating the activities into your lifestyle now, so you will be well prepared when the need arises.

AROUSAL-DECREASING ACTIVITIES:

- Bubble baths/hot tubs
- Warm showers
- Relaxing music
- Leisurely walks
- Light exercise
- Repetition of the word "Calm" or some other soothing mantra
- A warm blanket
- Oil painting, watercoloring or drawing
- Creative writing
- Gardening
- Movies (certain types)
- Hobbies (certain types)
- Cooking

- Soft lighting

- Pets

- Warm milk

- A complex-carbohydrate snack (popcorn, pretzels, etc.)

- Bio-feedback

- Massage

- Self-hypnosis

- Progressive relaxation techniques

- Meditation

- Visualize tranquil scenes

- Herbal tea

- Acupressure or Acupuncture

- Fishing

- Books (certain types)

- Television (certain programs)

- Positive affirmations

- Naps

- Yoga

- Slow, relaxed breathing

- Journal writing/daily diary

- Nurturing conversations

- A leisurely drive

- Focusing on the here and now

AROUSAL-INCREASING ACTIVITIES:

- Lively music

- Dancing

- Games

- Cold showers

- Rigorous exercise

- Spectator sports

- Participating in team sports

- Laughter

- Movies (certain types)

- Sky diving

- Para-sailing

- Hang-gliding

- Water or snow skiing

- Biking

- Singing

- Socializing

- Debating

- Sweet or spicy foods

- Sex

- Brisk walks

- Fresh air

- Driving fast

- Stimulating conversation

- Amusement parks

- A cool environment

There will naturally be times when the goal is neither to increase or decrease arousal, but rather to just divert attention -- healthy ways of changing channels. Sometimes the diversion is needed to avoid negative thoughts and feelings, other times it helps you become creatively involved in life. This list of non-addictive diversions is just a start, and many of the entries may coincide with the lists above. In time you will want to add some of your own ideas.

- Painting

- Drawing

- Writing

- Gardening

- Swimming

- Taking a class

- Cooking

- Attending a club, or group meeting

- Volunteer work

- Sculpting

- Photography

- Any type of physical activity

- Spectator sports

- Repair work

NEW F.A.N. WORKSHEET

FEELINGS + NEW ACTIONS = NEW FEELINGS

FEELINGS	+	NEW ACTIONS	=	NEW FEELINGS
Tension, Anxiety		HOT TUB		Feel Relaxed
Fears, Painful Memories		PLAY TENNIS		Forget uncomfortableness
Depression		GARDEN		Feel optimistic, Increase self-worth
Anger, Frustration		JOG ALONG THE OCEAN		Anger gone/diminished
Insomnia		TAKE A HOT SHOWER		Get to sleep
Boredom		WORK ON NEW HOBBY		Feel creative
Exhaustion, Tired		TAKE A BRISK WALK AROUND BLOCK		Feel energized
Thirsty, Hungry		EAT FRUIT OR VEGETABLES		Quench thirst, Feel satisfied
Marital Problems		GO SEE A MARRIAGE COUNSELOR		Feel loved and accepted
Low Self-esteem		WORK-OUT AT GYM		Feel better about self, Confident
Shyness, Social Inhibition		TAKE A DANCE CLASS		Feel socially at ease
Social Pressure		SIGN UP FOR AN ACTING WORKSHOP		Feel accepted by others
Internal Urge		LEARN YOGA		Relieve cravings
Loneliness		VOLUNTEER WORK		Feel connected and loved by people
SADNESS		GO TO A "FUNNY" MOVIE		FEEL HAPPY
WANT TO DRINK ALCOHOL		ATTEND A SUPPORT GROUP MEETING		STAY SOBER

183

NEW F.A.N. WORKSHEET

FEELINGS + NEW ACTIONS = NEW FEELINGS

FEELINGS	NEW ACTIONS	NEW FEELINGS
Tension, Anxiety		Feel Relaxed
Fears, Painful Memories		Forget uncomfortableness
Depression		Feel optimistic, Increase self-worth
Anger, Frustration		Anger gone/diminished
Insomnia		Get to sleep
Boredom		Feel creative
Exhaustion, Tired		Feel energized
Thirsty, Hungry		Quench thirst, Feel satisfied
Marital Problems		Feel loved and accepted
Low Self-esteem		Feel better about self, Confident
Shyness, Social Inhibition		Feel socially at ease
Social Pressure		Feel accepted by others
Internal Urge		Relieve cravings
Loneliness		Feel connected and loved by people

184

- Reading

- Any kind of hobby

- Mini-vacation or over-night getaway

- Movies, theatres, or concerts

- Puzzles

- Any type of building project

When you see a chance to change yourself by trying new non-destructive behaviors, JUST DO IT! You need to decide which strategy is the right one in each instance. It is my belief that if you look inside yourself, you will find the answer -- for when you understand them properly, feelings can be your best friend and guide.

CHAPTER 5 DEVELOPING YOUR NEW HEALTHY HABITS--FOCUSING ON YOU

PART 3 DEALING WITH PEOPLE--OUR SOCIAL ENVIRONMENT

As you will remember, one of the corners of the Pyramid of Change and Growth represents social and environmental forces. This chapter will help you understand the powerful role they play in your long-term recovery from unhealthy habits.

The goal is to learn to intervene against these environmental forces in order to change the way you think, behave and feel about yourself, and also to use them to alter the chemical and biological forces. As we have discussed, you will need as many strategies as possible in order to make an effective and lasting transition from your unhealthy habits to a new lifestyle.

Few issues that we have discussed so far will have as much influence on your habits as social and environmental factors. Whether you agree or not with the Alcoholics Anonymous philosophy, one thing it undeniably offers is a sober, encouraging social environment. If you are going to give up your unhealthy habits, it is imperative that you create your own healthy environment.

SELECTING A GROUP

As I have said before, 'no man is an island unto himself.' Your behavior is affected by others, and in turn your behavior affects other people with whom you associate. If you are a person who gambles too much or over-drinks, it is obviously wise to start socializing with non-gamblers and non-drinkers in an environment where these activities seldom or never take place.

You will need to find a group that strongly encourages you not to focus on old habits. Since the forces behind your unhealthy habit are so powerful, especially in the beginning when withdrawal symptoms and ingrained thinking patterns still have a strong hold, it is helpful to find a social support group that is inconsistent with your unhealthy habits.

If you choose Alcoholics Anonymous, which is a traditional 12-step program, you will find an accepting atmosphere as well as boundaries and direction. The people, the meetings and the philosophies will wrap you up and carry you along in a new social environmental atmosphere. Hopefully, you will be able to stick with it long enough to make a permanent transition.

Unfortunately, your options in Alcoholic's Anonymous along with other 12-step programs, are somewhat limited. The only choice that you have in these groups is lifelong attendance and acceptance of the 12-step philosophy. I happen to believe that AA and other 12-step type groups provide wonderful avenues for change, and I encourage you to avail yourself of their help if the 12-step programs meet your needs. There is an old saying which may apply with the 12-step methods: "Just take what you want and leave the rest." This may be difficult to do because if you don't follow the program, like a road map, you can easily get off course and become lost again. If you have tried 12-step programs, and they just don't work for you, then you must seek out an avenue of your own that will support your health and continued growth.

In addition to the traditional 12-step programs there are several other new national organizations that you may find helpful. Below, is a partial listing of Addiction-Focused groups:

• RATIONAL RECOVERY (RR) -- This is a national, abstinence-based, free, self-help support group based on Rational-Emotive Therapy as developed by Albert Ellis, Ph.D. There are separate groups for alcohol, drugs, and overeating. I highly recommend this organization whose focus is learning to identify and change the thinking that leads to practicing unhealthy habits.

• SECULAR ORGANIZATION FOR SOBRIETY (SOS) -- This is another national, abstinence-based, free, self-help group for those with alcohol related problems.

• WOMEN FOR SOBRIETY (WFS) -- This is a national abstinence-based, free self-help group serving only women with alcohol problems.

If none of these organizations seem suited to your needs, be assured that there are many other local and community groups from which to choose. Your local newspaper is probably the best source of listings. You will find groups that deal exclusively with bad habits while others might focus on common interests. Whatever the group is, if you feel it can help you by keeping you from engaging in your habit, then by all means sign-up. Make sure that you work within the group to develop friendships that can provide sound structures satisfy your feelings of loneliness, isolation, and change the thinking that "you are the only person with the problem."

If you choose not to use a pre-established support group, then get involved in university classes, church activities or other organizations listed in your local newspaper. Even bridge, chess, or sailing clubs can provide structures and diversion, and give you something to look forward to that is new and exciting. The bottom line is that you must develop social relationships with friends, loved ones, and perhaps therapists who genuinely support you and really want you to make a change. You must keep these people in your life

These people are part of your success! Do not discard them after you start to do better and are feeling more confident. Hold on to them, as they are on your team and sincerely want you to continue your success.

DO NOT ISOLATE YOURSELF!

We need healthy relationships to encourage growth, development and the expression of individuality. In my clinical experience, no one has succeeded in conquering an unhealthy habit totally alone. More often than not, most people with serious unhealthy habits spend much of their time alone, engaging in their unhealthy shortcut-life behavior. They often refer to alcohol, food, drugs, cigarettes, or other habits as their 'best friend.' When this "friend" is gone, they are going to need a replacement.

If you are an "isolator," this is a MAJOR part of the problem. You simply cannot make it without reaching out to people. I realize that it is sometimes very difficult to break through those barriers and establish lines of trust. But, you cannot overcome your long-standing habits without that trusting type of relationship in your life. Even if you feel extremely uncomfortable around people, it is in your best interest to get socially involved whenever possible. If you structure your life so you are seldom alone, it will be that much harder for you to engage in your unhealthy habit.

Social connections serve another purpose as well -- unless you find that recovery is more fun than your unhealthy habit, the change will not last. Supportive friends do more than just "catch" us like a safety net; they also help us build strong and loving relationships, which provide us with a deeply satisfying sense of emotional connection. They help us have fun and give us something we can share and experience together.

189

SHY?

If shyness is a problem for you, take a hard look at yourself and determine what you can do to overcome it. Don't just leave the problem on the back burner with a promise of 'someday' I'll change. FIX IT NOW!! If you don't think you can do it alone, it may be useful to seek some therapy -- either individual or group. Many people practicing unhealthy habits tend to reject others, and in turn feel rejected themselves. You need to change so you can connect!

You must try to determine what it is that prevents you from developing these positive connections. If you have suffered in the past, it is understandable that you will be extra sensitive and distrustful. You need to find the courage to overcome these feelings or chance are you will never conquer your habit. "Not relating well" will keep you isolated -- away from the positive groups and activities that are so vital to your recovery from your unhealthy lifestyle habits.

JOYCE

When Joyce came to me at the age of twenty-five, her life orbited around constant exercise with as little food intake per day as possible. The wife of a very successful attorney, she had given up her job as an advertising account executive when their first child was born. Even though her life was filled with constant activity all day long, tending to the needs of a newborn baby, she somehow felt unfulfilled, empty, and constantly searching for something. She had lost the definition of who she was in her own mind. Over the first few months of adjusting to her new life at home, she found it convenient just to skip lunch and devote all of her time to the baby and the house. She discovered that this new hectic lifestyle partially replaced the fast-paced lifestyle she had become accustomed to on her former job. She also found that she had time to focus a little more on herself. She thought that this would be the perfect opportunity to "tone herself up" and develop a more athletic look. Soon she had bought a motorized treadmill, an air-bike, a rowing machine, hand weights, exercise clothes, and a whole array of other exercise equipment. She would even jog around the house while doing the housework and tending to the baby. Before long, her whole life centered around exercise and child care. She no longer had time for any of her friends, and she always saw herself as being just a little too fat and "puny" which motivated her to become more and more athletic -- devoted to a regiment of almost constant exercise.

Being always exhausted, she had no time for her husband and had developed a cranky and irritable attitude. Finally, her husband confronted her, and after a much heated discussion, forced her to admit that all the exercise and starvation was attempting to fill the place of the loneliness and the feelings of lack of accomplishment in her life.

When she came to me, we started stretching her "life envelope." I suggested that she reconnect with her old friends in the neighborhood along with some of her favorite people at her old job. I recommended that she curtail her strenuous regiment of exercise, and instead, join a ballroom dancing class with her husband. That would allow her to get the proper amount of exercise while connecting in a very positive and romantic way with her husband.

I sent her to her physician for a complete physical examination and then to a professional nutritionalist to re-establish proper eating habits.

Although it was very difficult for her, she cooperated and soon found that she did have a fulfilling mission in life after all. Constant exercise became less and less important and she was able to focus on other ways of feeling good again. Her connections with her old friends and her husband (not isolating herself any longer), along with her ability to focus on "life as it truly is," instead of focusing on "life as she imagined it to be" was the all important key to her success.

CONNECTIONS

Have you ever been on a team (baseball, bowling, football, soccer, etc.) where the members have developed such close-knit teamwork that you almost know what the other person is going to do before he/she does it. When we really connect with other people, we experience a sort of emotional rhythm. Even though this bond is not verbally acknowledged, we tend to feel safe and able to be vulnerable, as though we can express ourself without fear of criticism. This non-verbal interaction is crucial to our happiness and is necessary if we are to give up our unhealthy habits. Without at least one or two people in our lives with whom we can experience this type of connection, we are left feeling alone and discouraged.

The reasons we fail to connect with others are complex. Most often, it stems back to childhood where our role models themselves may have been uncomfortable with intimacy. Or perhaps in the past, we were wounded rather than rewarded for our attempts at openness. The foundation for our ability to relate well with others begins early in life, sometimes just after birth. For example, if your mother was depressed or not available to you at this early stage, your social skills did not have a chance to develop properly. If the pattern continued into childhood, over time you likely concluded that the best and safest route was to lock people out.

Such strategies rely exclusively on walling yourself off from everything and everybody. That is precisely why you turned to your unhealthy habits, to soothe your loneliness and isolation. It is a strategy you must abandon now, if you hope to connect in any real way. Sometimes, it takes a good therapist to slowly help you learn to trust and to understand exactly how you fail to connect with others. Your therapist may assist you in realizing that you respond to the same destructive kinds of connections you experienced as a child. This is why some people tend to repeat marrying the same type of wife or husband, over and over again. You must learn to let healthy people into your life if you are to fully satisfy your needs.

When you become accustomed to practicing some kind of unhealthy lifestyle habit, you don't feel the need to connect with other people. If you go "one-on-one" with your unhealthy habit, you find it the easiest of all relationships -- it is predictable and non-demanding. But, sooner or later, during logical/rational moments you are left feeling lonely and empty, yearning for the "real thing."

Do yourself a favor -- start searching for a friend with whom you can make an emotional connection. It will probably take time and the journey will not always be smooth. It will be tempting to choose the first person who seems to understand. It is important to be patient, and make sure that his/her behavior is consistent and worthy of a long-term emotional investment on your part.

You must have the strength and the determination to reach out and learn how to use people as positive structures. Evaluate yourself honestly. If you seem to repel people you would like to know better, try to understand what you are doing that makes you unattractive to them. Life is too short and very lonely at times, but you can overcome your emotional "two left feet" and connect with those who will give you hope, meaning and support.

BOUNDARIES

Boundaries are the other side of connecting. There is an invisible line between you and another person that is difficult to describe. Upon first entering therapy, many of my clients seem to have no sense of boundaries at all. It is almost as if they do not know where they end and I begin. As a result, their style of relating with other people borders on the extreme. Either they intrude inappropriately into the lives of friends and loved ones or else their own boundaries are nonexistent and they let others influence their moods, dictate their feelings and control their lives. This is the other end of the spectrum from individuals whose boundaries are so rigid that they don't permit any connections at all.

A healthy balance lies somewhere between these extremes. In order to understand and define your own boundaries or lack of them, you need to carefully analyze each of your relationships. As you do so you will realize that they differ with each person, whether they are spouses, children, parents, friends, business colleagues, lovers, employers, or employees.

It is important that you understand the significance of boundaries, for they are a vital part of the dynamics of any relationship. Without a healthy sense of limits, it is impossible to establish and maintain healthy involvements. If someone close to you is overstepping an unstated boundary, it is normal for you to be angry and it is acceptable to verbalize those feelings. Conversely, if it is you who are not sensitive to the boundaries of others, you may find yourself the target of resentment. One way to deal with this is to ask each of the people in your life exactly what they are comfortable with, and then you must decide exactly where you want to draw the line with each of them.

NICK

Nick was struggling with a drinking problem and was already in his forties, but he had no more idea of how to set boundaries than a child. He had a manipulative mother who used her frequent bouts of ill health and alleged financial problems as an excuse to call him at all hours of the night and intrude into his personal life. Never having learned to say 'no' to his mother, he had little success in drawing the line with the other women in his life.

His ex-wife demanded his time and extra cash whenever she experienced problems, and his current girlfriend often extended and accepted invitations without consulting him. These patterns existed for so long that he had no real understanding of appropriate behavior. He only knew that he felt constantly and hopelessly pressured.

After a few discussions with me about what constitutes acceptable boundaries, he finally understood the concept of setting limits. "It seems simple now, and I feel a little foolish for not realizing it sooner. I suppose because my mother never respected boundaries, I got used to people charging in from every direction," he explained.

The only way Nick had been able to limit the uncomfortable intrusions was to "barricade himself" with alcohol. Once inside that blissful fog, he could block out the world and sometimes,if he was drunk enough, he could even muster the courage to say "no."

Learning to say no when he was sober, on a regular basis, was a difficult but important first step for him. He started by asking his mother, his ex-wife, and his girlfriend to respect the new limits that he was setting. At first, they did not take him seriously -- they even became a little angry at him, and continued their normal patterns. At times Nick would "give-in," as he was so used to his old behavior. "I can't stand them being angry with me." "When they get upset it hurts me."

As he slowly learned how to say "no," he established boundaries between their needs and his. He began to gain a sense of control over his life. As the pressure eased and he was able to create some genuine comfort zones, the need for alcohol as a safe haven became less seductive and less of an option.

Boundaries are often disregarded under the guise of "helpfulness," especially in the case of overprotective parents. Although it is difficult to reestablish limits after a long-term pattern has been in force, it is not too late to start the process of change. I'm not suggesting that you jolt your loved ones by suddenly erecting an impenetrable wall; however, you need to determine what you want in each relationship, and the make friends and family aware of your feelings. You can do this with a personal encounter or by a tactfully written letter letting everyone know that you are changing your life for the better by setting boundaries.

I once had a client from a very wealthy family that had no understanding of boundaries. Sandy's mother was unusually talented in many areas and would insist on "helping" her decorate her room, decide which classes to take, how to dress, and what friends to have. Consequently, Sandy failed to develop self-reliance, personal tastes, and any sense of who she was. The moment she faltered her mother was there to stepin. In doing so, the parent undermined the development of her daughter and established an unhealthy habit of dependency that continued well into Sandy's adulthood. Over time, Sandy's self-esteem and confidence never really developed, and she entered a state where she could not think for herself. Feeling so unsure of herself in so many areas, the only "control" she found was the control of food in her life. As a result, she started on the roller coaster ride known as Anorexia.

You will need to develop a new sensitivity to others, as well as, to your own emotional needs. You must also determine when your limits are so rigid that they restrict or diminish relationships with other people. You will need to look back over your life and assess past as well as current connections in terms of healthy and respectful boundaries for everyone concerned.

CARRYING YOUR OWN ROCKS!

In teaching boundaries, there is a concept that I refer to as "Carrying Your Own Rocks." So many people who practice unhealthy habits seem to go through life with their arms stretched out, waiting for other people to load them down with their "rocks." This co-dependent style is learned in childhood when some of us are taught to become "people-pleasers." We always feel the need to be "up" or "on-stage" so that our parents and others won't be let down by us. We have been trained to please others with total disregard for ourselves which forces us to put on an act for others. People-pleasers think that others must always see them as being happy, understanding, and willing to help. People-pleasers develop guilt if they don't take on other people's problems, even at the expense of their own mental and physical stability. This is not an easy pattern to change, but it is imperative that you learn to let others "Carry Their Own Rocks" so that you will have the time and energy to tend to your own needs.

I'm not encouraging you to become cold, uncaring and self-centered. I suggest that you put your energy into dealing with your own concerns first and foremost. Do your loved ones, your friends, and yourself a big favor: listen, suggest, support, encourage, and love them, but let them handle their own problems and "Carry Their Own Rocks" around.

You are reading this book to help yourself take control and develop healthy habits. As you use the tools it offers, you will likely find that many relationships and behaviors are not in your best interest. You may come to realize that one or more of your involvements with other people is abusive or even that your job is unnecessarily stressful for your good health. For example, if you are living or associating closely with another person who is abusive to you, overprotective, dominating and controlling you -- or if your job is

Don't accept rocks from others —
only carry your own.

emotionally draining, unsatisfying, full of pressure and stress put upon you by a boss or a system that cares nothing for you as a human being with rights -- then there is probably little chance of you giving up your unhealthy habits as they have become your "secret safety zone" that protects you from life's unpleasantries.

You will have to develop the courage to make a big decision, take a big step, and make the proper plans that will allow you to cut those ties -- even if it means moving to another city, or seeking new employment, or developing an entirely new group of friends. Though it may cause initial stress, with proper planning, the long-term benefits are definitely worth it!

Remember our motto: "Don't Kill Yourself, Skill Yourself."

CHAPTER 5 DEVELOPING YOUR NEW HEALTHY HABITS--FOCUSING ON YOU

PART 4 CHANGING YOUR FEELINGS DIRECTLY

The fourth and last corner of the Pyramid of Change and Growth is BIOCHEMISTRY. You may be wondering just what that means and how it applies. You should know that it is perhaps the most important of the corners of change. In fact, when I was creating this model, I considered putting biochemistry at the top of the Pyramid instead of feelings, because feelings are technically nothing more than a sensation caused by a change in our brain chemistry. As we have seen, this alteration can be the result of our thinking, our actions or our social environment. Biochemistry differs from the other factors in that it can be changed directly without going through these other channels. To some degree you have been effecting such changes all your life without realizing it. Now, you are going to learn how to alter your biochemistry at will, as a vital part of your recovery from practicing unhealthy habits.

If you have been using your unhealthy habit to avoid being uncomfortable, to get high, or to feel better, then you have been pushing your biochemical buttons for years, in a negative way. Now, you are going to learn how to do it in a way that is healthy and positive. It is important that you have a good understanding of the biochemical influences which cause discomfort, and consequently propel you toward practicing your unhealthy habits. You should also know that all habits have biochemistry-changing properties. If you are a compulsive shopper, a gambler, or a workaholic, there is a euphoria that occurs which is a result of you changing your chemistry -- much like a "runner's high."

Understanding this concept will give you the knowledge and power to conquer your habit, be it physical or psychological in origin. In this chapter, we will discuss several methods you can easily incorporate into your daily routine.

As a beginning, I encourage each of you to have a physical exam that includes a test for hypoglycemia. This one disorder has been at the root of many of my client's problems. It may explain why you crave sugar, in the form of food or alcohol, and why you sometimes suffer mood swings, depression, and fatigue. Fortunately, this condition can be corrected through dietary changes. If you test positive, you would be wise to consult a nutritionist. If your craving includes alcohol, be sure to ask your physician for a liver function reading.

DIET

Changing your diet is simple for the short run and "on the surface." However, I believe that it is the hardest habit to change permanently, because it is our foundation for changing all of our feelings and is the basis for all other habits. Remember, the very first time you cried as an infant, your mother fed you to comfort you. At that moment, you came to learn, on a very primal level, about the connections between food intake, biochemical changes, and feelings. When you do alter your diet, it is the easiest and most direct way to achieve prompt results in changing mood and/or feelings.

You already know that too much caffeine and sugar are not good for you, but you may not have connected their use to the problem of unhealthy habits. These quick-fix substances are a way to "press buttons" when you are not comfortable with the way you feel. The trouble is when you load up on coffee or sweets to soothe your mood, you are setting yourself up to go right back to your bad habit. The lifts they produce are short in length and soon leave you feeling even lower than before.

Whether you use a substance or a behavior as a bad habit, you are failing to face the real problem. Quick fixes bypass the real problem and the old vicious cycle is perpetuated. When you learn to alter your diet in a constructive way, you will feel better in the long-run and that will set-off a chain of positive side benefits.

This is not meant to be a "Diet Book" as so much can be stated about that topic, but a book centered around the development of healthy habits. But, here are a few helpful suggestions:

- Reduce your caffeine intake.

- Eliminate or drastically reduce your use of sugars.

- Eat several small meals a day instead of three large ones.

- Never allow yourself to become overly hungry.

MEDICATIONS

I am a strong believer in the appropriate use of psychiatric drugs by individuals who are genetically predisposed to depression, panic attacks, manic-depressive mood swings, thought disorders, and hyperactivity. Years ago there was no remedy, but today there are a number of effective medications to help you. To suffer alone is needless and even more important, these kinds of unrelenting symptoms can provoke and compound the problem of practicing unhealthy habits.

While alleviating the symptoms may not in itself bring an end to compulsive behavior, it is the first important step. Once you can function without genetic or biological shackles, your chances of altering your lifestyle and overcoming bad habits are dramatically increased. If you suffer from any extreme form of the above disorders, or if you have unrelenting insomnia, contact a psychiatrist today. There are medications, all non-addicting, that when used properly, can make a substantial improvement in the quality of your life.

I feel a special need to say something about depression. Most of my clients have to some degree battled with this demon. This common disorder is manifested by inability to sleep, reduced sexual desire, significant changes in weight, a sense of hopelessness and helplessness, and a general lack of energy. It is my opinion that a great many people have been seduced into unhealthy habits to help overcome depression. Naturally, such solutions are short-lived and can actually cause the condition to worsen. If you are suffering from depression, see a doctor. After a thorough physical examination, discuss with him the possibility of trying one of the newer non-addicting anti-depressants. These drugs will not make you "high," but they will relieve your sense of despair. I have seen remarkable results from their appropriate utilization.

Other symptoms can also be relieved or reduced with proper medication -- excessive energy, confused non-connected thinking, poor concentration, obsessive/compulsive behaviors and lack of impulse control. In addition, there are special drugs for those who want extra help in abstaining from alcohol or narcotic use, for sexual compulsions, or for relief from detoxification symptoms.

VITAMINS AND OVER-THE-COUNTER DRUGS

In addition to providing insurance against improper nutrition, megadoses of vitamins and amino acids are sometimes used to alleviate depression and even phobias. This is a relatively new field and still somewhat controversial. If you decide to avail yourself of vitamin therapy, by all means consult your physician, a nutritionist, bookstore, and/or library to acquaint yourself with the negative, along with the positive aspects. It is advisable to make yourself very aware of how megadoses of various vitamins can affect your body both in a productive and adverse way.

If you try over-the-counter medications such as sleep or diet aids, consult your physician, and make sure you don't take them as a solution in themselves. You should use them only as a part of a well-balanced sleep/hygiene program or long-term eating plan.

HOLISTIC METHODS

Another area which falls outside the realm of traditional medicine is the "holistic approach," which includes: Acupuncture, Acupressure, Herbology, Chiropractic, and various Eastern Methodologies only recently accepted in Western Society. You can consider these approaches as ways of affecting your biochemistry directly. If you become proactive and these therapies seem to provide you with benefits and make it easier for you to refrain from your short-cut solutions, then make them a part of your life.

As with vitamins, the more education you have the better off you are; and it pays to remind yourself of the old adage, "A little knowledge is a dangerous thing." Many herbs are known for their healing and invigorating properties; however, taken indiscriminately, they can be dangerous. For some people, herbs have harmful side-affects. Just because something is labeled as being "natural" does not mean that it is automatically benign. This is not to discourage you from the use of such methodologies, but I strongly urge you to do a lot of studying about any therapy you plan to pursue, and to consult your physician.

DETOXIFICATION

As you begin to break away from your destructive relationships with your unhealthy habits, you will go through a period of detoxification. This detoxification can be both mental and physical. The process involves withdrawal symptoms resulting from the removal of the unhealthy substance or activity from your life. It is often very difficult, if not impossible, to distinguish between physical and psychological withdrawal symptoms. During the 'detox' period it is almost certain that you will feel uncomfortable. There is no way to dodge that bullet and many people use it as an excuse to return to their unhealthy habits, or simply to not quit at all. Being able to utilize some of the tools in this and other chapters will help you deal with these discomforts in a direct fashion. Dealing in a direct fashion can be vital to you overcoming your unhealthy habits.

Detoxification time is variable from person to person. In most instances of alcohol or cigarette habits, detoxing can take only a couple of days, or at most a few weeks. However, habits that revolve around drugs or food can stretch from six months to a year. For some drugs, there is a period of secondary withdrawal that begins after three to six months of abstinence. Without this knowledge, it is all too easy to misinterpret distressing symptoms as reasons to return to your old patterns.

Don't be frightened by these physical symptoms (although you should always make your physician a part of this process); they will usually subside if you "hang in there" and don't resume your habit. While there are prescription medications which provide relief, the vast majority of people over-dramatize their sensations and use false conditions as excuses for returning to old habits. Your task is to use the tools in this book (approved for you by your physician) and your new environment, so you can resist that temptation.

Last of all, remember that much of the power you give these uncomfortable feelings function as your beliefs about those feelings. Go back and reread the section about "Changing Your Thinking." Also, recognize that more people relapse due to psychological rather than physiological symptoms. Chances are if you are still suffering after a few months of abstinence, it is not because you remain physically dependent, but because you are still dependent in your mind.

Remember, "You Must Skill Yourself, Not Kill Yourself!"

CHAPTER 6 SOME THINGS JUST ARE

PART 1 I HAVE NO CONTROL OVER THAT

"It is a far, far better thing that I do, than I have ever done. . . "
This closing passage from Charles Dickens' novel, "A Tale of Two Cities," captures the
spirit of what you are currently and actively doing to develop new healthy habits. This is
perhaps the most positive and constructive decision that you have ever made for yourself and
about yourself in your entire life. You are establishing a new life that is both more
rewarding, and more happy -- one that gives you more control.

I realize that the concept of "limited control" is difficult to understand and accept,
because many of us have built a life around the concept that we need to be in complete
charge, total control. Control after all, is a defense against fear. In many instances, taking
charge or just "trying harder" does enable us to overcome many of life's hurdles.

You finished school, you got the job, you presided over a special project, and very
often, got all or most of the praise for making a "great effort." The problem is this
technique has worked to a certain extent and you have become comfortable with it.
However, it does not work all or even most of the time, and it doesn't apply in many
important areas of life. There are just so many areas in life where, in spite of our best
efforts, we just don't have control.

The famous Alcoholic's Anonymous "Serenity Prayer" goes something like this:
"Grant me the serenity to accept the things that I cannot change, the courage to change the
things I can, and the wisdom to know the difference." This is a wonderful motto and serves
a good purpose. The only difficulty is that it does not spell out which things you can and

cannot change. That is the job of this section of the book. As we move along, remember that science and Psychology are always progressing, and those things we cannot control today, we MAY be able to manage better in the future.

Reviewing what we have discussed so far, we see that control is a central issue in all unhealthy habits. More specifically, as demonstrated by the F.A.N. model, we see that we are drawn to substances or behaviors that provide us with a sense of control over our feelings. This is perfectly normal, for knowing that we can change our emotional state at will makes us feel more secure. But problems arise when we encounter something unchangeable. When we have created a certain perception of ourselves based on the illusion of control, it is frightening when something comes along that evades our limited powers. Our response is likely to be anger, depression, or even a feeling of hopelessness.

You need a new attitude toward control. As the "Serenity Prayer" suggests, we need to come to terms with the fact that many things in life are simply beyond our control. Only when we understand and believe that fact do we truly have control in the broadest sense. It is the belief that you SHOULD be able to control a certain thing that makes you feel helpless -- when that certain thing cannot be controlled or is outside your sphere of control. On the other hand, when you have truly accepted that something is unchangeable, you can begin to rechannel your energies into a productive direction. For example, no one worries about what time the sun rises and sets, because of our lack of control.

The Alcoholics Anonymous method of handling an uncontrollable situation is to 'turn it over' to presumably a higher power or to God. What I would like each of you to do when you encounter a non-controllable situation or issue is to 'accept it, and let it go.' If you fail to do this, you will be on auto-pilot constantly beating your head against a wall that will

208

never crumble. It is time to realize that the wall is not going to move, your boss' personality is not going to change, you will not change the rules of society, your mother will not quit nagging you, and you will always have to pay taxes. None of this is your fault and none of it is in your sphere of control, so just "let it go" and stop destroying yourself over issues that even your best efforts cannot fix.

Granted, you will have to overcome the Madison Avenue mind set that tells us that we should be able to control just about everything. It simply is not true and it will never be true. Even the President of the United States cannot control everything. He is not a Dictator or an absolute Autocrat. He finds his sphere of control has definite boundaries even though he has an immense amount of power and influence. The sooner you give up the child-like position that you can accomplish anything and control everything, the sooner you will find peace of mind and emotional resilience.

I realize that I am asking you to give up a technique that you have used all your life to protect yourself from real and imagined dangers. You must learn that "life is what it is and not what you want it to be." At some point you are going to die and nothing can prevent it. If you accept the fact that you can change certain things in life but not others, then you are in as much control of your life as anyone can possibly be.

SOME THINGS JUST ARE!

Lets take a hard look together at some of the things that are beyond anyone's control. The actual list would be endless, but here are some things we all have to live with:

- YOUR BASIC PHYSICAL APPEARANCE. Even though surgeons and beauticians can do remarkable things, in the end we still look like ourselves. We will not look like a new person that nobody will recognize, it will always be us. We must learn to live with our height, our bone structure, our body types, and our features.

- GENETIC PREDISPOSITION. Our basic temperament, physical and intellectual limitations, and susceptibility to certain diseases. These are all things that we are "stuck with."

- CHILDHOOD TRAUMAS. The pain our parents, relatives, and friends caused, including divorce, incest, child abuse, rape, death of loved ones, accidents, etc.

- THE WEATHER AND OTHER ACTS OF NATURE. We plan prudently, but we cannot have sunshine on demand. We cannot predict or prevent earthquakes, floods, fires, tornados, or storms.

- MAN-MADE MISTAKES. We can allow ourselves ample time and preparation, but we cannot control the flow of traffic, the long lines at the store, or mechanical break-downs.

- THE POLITICAL AND ECONOMIC CLIMATE. We can vote for the person of our choice, donate time and money to good causes, but in the broad scope of politics and the economy, the real decision-making power is out of our hands.

- OTHER PEOPLE'S MOODS AND BEHAVIOR PATTERNS. We can hope that others will respond to us favorably, but we cannot dictate how our children will ultimately behave away from home or control the mood of a "traffic cop."

- YOUR MATE'S HABITS AND IDIOSYNCRASIES. We can make the best possible choice in partners, but we cannot control what they think and do.

- HEALTH, OUR OWN OR THAT OF OTHERS. We can live the healthiest possible lifestyle and encourage our loved ones to do the same, but there are some health factors that none of us can control.

- GAMES OF CHANCE. In spite of some dreamers' unshakable belief in the "sure thing," if any of us could control the outcome of games of chance, they would cease to exist.

- PARENTS. I am sure if we could choose our parents, we all would design people who would fit our mood, needs and temperament the best. However, just as in games of chance, you have no control over the outcome of who your parents are, how wealthy or intelligent they are, or how they treat us.

- DEATH. Creating unusual euphemisms for death is where our control begins and ends.

As we see, those areas in our life we can control are far fewer than most of us would like. If your only technique for dealing with fear or building self-esteem is to try to exert control, you are in great danger of returning to your unhealthy habit for the rest of your life. If on the other hand, you can accept the fact that much of life is beyond your control and learn to "let it go," when letting go is the best or the only thing you can do, then you are far less likely to seek out the false comfort of the quick-fix.

Each of us is handicapped in some way, and it does no good to spend our entire lives bemoaning those aspects we cannot change. All we can do is look at the half-full side of our lives, the parts that we can control, and do something positive with our time and energy. Our lives can be as "rich" or as "poor" as we choose to make them.

A balanced lifestyle is one key to
health and happiness.

FINDING BALANCE

Finding peace from the torment of destructive behavior requires the creation of balance in your life. A balanced lifestyle means recognizing those things we can and cannot change, and learning to stay balanced within these two factors.

As we discussed in the "Five Finger Exercise," you need to "get a life" -- by that we mean one that is well-rounded. To accomplish this, you need to develop a life filled with activities that give each day meaning and purpose. Doing so will enable you to derive fulfillment from those things you can change, so that it will be easier to let go of things which you cannot change.

A balanced lifestyle includes MANY elements in addition to merely giving up an unhealthy habit. If you are currently unemployed, go out and find some sort of work. If your job is not rewarding, put energy into getting a better one. If your primary relationship is troubled, work on improving it. If change doesn't seem possible, then find a new relationship which has real potential. Commit yourself to volunteer work, get involved in creative projects, join a ball club or offer to coach a team. Make physical activities and leisure time a part of your everyday life, so you do not become just a workaholic.

The broader the base of your interests and activities, and the more you derive pleasure from a variety of things, the more stable your recovery from unhealthy habits will be. You cannot remain centered if your energy is focused into one or two areas. Merely substituting one habit for another does not work. Many people give up drinking only to become workaholics, while others go from gambling to overspending. A return to any singular method as a way of coping will only set you up for a relapse.

Probably the toughest issue we face in dealing with change and acceptance is knowing when it is more productive to "let it go" and move to another area where we can have greater impact and rewards. The challenge occurs when you encounter a situation that you can influence only to a degree. Perhaps you are able to talk your spouse or companion into getting therapy; or perhaps your relationship is so deeply troubled that at best, it will be only tolerable. Finding balance involves knowing when it is worthwhile, and when it is not, to expend your time and energy.

Finding balance means learning to distinguish between a situation worth fighting for and one that is a lost cause. It means having a broad enough base that you can derive more pleasure from a new lifestyle than you did from your unhealthy behavior.

A basic principle to consider is this: "What truly reflects your best interests?" That doesn't mean choosing what feels the best or what is easiest or what is immediately attainable. If what you need is to change jobs, or move to another city, or end a tortured relationship, you must find the courage to do it. If you are convinced that it is better to stay in your current situation and work on resolving the problems, then that is the course you must take.

TAKE CONTROL NOW!

CHAPTER 6 SOME THINGS JUST ARE

PART 2 THE BEST IS YET TO BE (Confronting Common Problems in Changing Habits)

The following items are some specific areas that have consistently been found to be difficult for some people to deal with when breaking their unhealthy habits. Each item is intended to be an introduction into the specific topic rather than being an all-inclusive discussion. Remember, it is your life and if you are being held back by a particular problem, take control and solve it. Once you overcome the final "bumps in the road"; you will discover the "best is yet to be" -- your life will be more enjoyable, rewarding, and satisfying without the burden of your unhealthy habit. For years you have carried the burden of your unhealthy habit. It has been as though you were constantly holding a sack filled with sand. The more you focused on your unhealthy habit and the more you practiced it, the heavier the sack of sand became. Once you leave your unhealthy habits behind, it is like putting down the sack of sand -- what relief and joy to rid yourself of something so non-productive and tiring. How happy you will be not to focus so much of your life on carrying around a heavy sack of sand that contributes nothing to your life. Freedom is a wonderful thing that allows you to explore all kinds of positive new opportunities. The best is truly yet to be, so enjoy it to the maximum.

SLEEP

One of the most common rationalizations I hear from people wanting to return to their unhealthy habits is lack of sleep. People say to me: "I HAVE to function! I have to do my job and it takes sleep to perform properly!" Or, "If I don't take a Valium tonight, I'm going to lose my job because I will be so nervous I won't be able to cope with the job stress."

It is important that you do not give in on this issue. Even if it takes a night, a week, or a month of not sleeping well. It is a normal state of transition and it WILL go away as you relearn your coping skills. You need to remember that your biochemistry has been disrupted from years of relying on your unhealthy habit. Psychologically, you have forgotten what it takes to let go and fall asleep naturally. The only way that you are going to relearn how to fall asleep and let your biochemistry get back to normal is to NOT engage in your unhealthy habit. It is important to understand and expect this initial insomnia and not to read it as something going wrong. You are breaking your cycle and your biochemistry is readapting.

It is true that you may function below your peak for a while, but get up in the morning and do your best the rest of the day. Stay awake and try to force yourself into sleeping only during the evening hours. If you cannot sleep at night, get up and read, watch television, do light housework, or very mild stretching exercises. Don't return to your unhealthy habit, it will only catapult you right back into your old vicious cycle.

This might be a good time to take a class in relaxation techniques or self-hypnosis. Perhaps try an audio tape that has relaxing music and encouraging messages recorded on it. Take charge of learning how to fall asleep -- make it your primary project. Use hot tubs, massage, yoga, chanting, anything that does not lead you down the path to your unhealthy habit again. If the sleep habit is persistent, see your physician or even a center for sleep disorders. Remember, do not fall back on your old unhealthy habit!

ARE YOU TRYING FOR PERFECTION?

This would be a good time to re-read the section about living with things that you cannot change. You can change some habits, but it is essential that you learn to "let go" and become more comfortable with the imperfect self that you are and need to accept.

This book could go on forever in terms of all the possible habits and behaviors that people want to change. Learning to accept your imperfections, your minor habits, is especially difficult for people who have the perception that they always need to be in control. Perfectionism is an unhealthy habit in itself when carried to extremes and it must be addressed like other unhealthy habits -- you need to strive for a reduction in this area as well.

Perfectionism is all too often a ploy or shield to protect yourself from fears of being abandoned, not loved, criticized, or embarrassed, or used as a defense mechanism so that people will leave you alone. You must learn that you are a Human Being and not a machine. Accept your imperfections and accept your Humanism. If you rely too heavily on the false illusion of protection through perfection, then you have set up a life for yourself of always fearing the slightest flaws, and you will create a greater fear of others, which will "drive you crazy"! All the self-help books, support groups and therapists will not make you perfect, so you must learn to live within your skin, with what you were given.

A special note: Some workplaces in today's overly complex and technical environment have come to expect too much from their employees. The corporate demand for perfectionism usually comes from those "up high" who are insulated from the day-to-day activities of the workplace. If you are in a job that is trying to make a "computer" out of you, it will be necessary for you to change your life in the following ways. You must establish in your mind that the goals set are impossible to live by, yet you must do your best to do your job in the most competent way that you can. It is good to interface with your co-workers and let your beliefs be known; however, it is important not to become a whiner or troublemaker. Just state the fact that you are a Human Being subject to fatigue, mis-understandings, confusion, and making mistakes. State that your job performance is important to you, and you know you were hired because the company had confidence that you could perform the job duties. From that point, "give yourself some slack" and forgive yourself for the mistakes you make. If you are criticized for those mistakes, consider the source and understand that those criticizing you are under the same burden of perfectionism that once burdened you.

Do not let an attitude of perfectionism in the workplace make you a workaholic. An overly tired worker is an inefficient worker and therefore makes more mistakes.

If the workplace is too perfectionistic, perhaps it is time to actively seek other employment with an organization that allows you to be the Human Being that you are.

Remember our motto: "Don't Kill Yourself, Skill Yourself." Perfectionism is a killer! Strive to make yourself a skilled component of the workplace while retaining your Humanity.

TIME AND MONEY MANAGEMENT

We have already discussed keeping a diary and learning how to structure your time. It is also important that you learn how to structure your finances, for they have a far-reaching effect on other areas of your life. If you find that you have been resistant to structuring either time or money, then you need to realize that this is a bad habit in itself.

If you cannot afford to hire a financial consultant, take a class in money management or get some books on money management from the library. Just make sure that you put yourself on some sort of program and stick to it! If you think you can get around this, you are being naive.

Even if you have dug yourself into a hole with gambling, shopping, or drug debts, you need to begin to take charge and turn the situation around. The money you have previously devoted to maintaining your unhealthy habits can now be used in your best interests. Now, you should have money available so you can join a health club, hire a fitness trainer, or retain a financial consultant. Perhaps you even have enough money that you can afford a Chiropractor, a massage series, or some other professional who can help you "put your life back together."

PROCRASTINATION

There is nothing which is more likely to lead us back to our unhealthy habits than PROCRASTINATION! Procrastination is founded on fear and the dread of doing something. Putting off the challenge of "facing the dragon" does not make that challenge or problem go away.

There is no easy way to break an unhealthy habit. The only way is to push through your barriers and overcome your tendency to procrastinate. When you enter unfamiliar and frightening territory and face your fears and dreads "head-on," you will not only increase your self-esteem but you will keep your fears from growing and multiplying.

LAPSE AND RELAPSE

A lapse is a single episode where you fall back on your unhealthy habit. There is nothing very alarming or wrong with that behavior. On the other hand, a relapse is a slipping back into your unhealthy behavior pattern just as before.

A lapse, and sometimes even a relapse, can provide a profound opportunity to develop new tools and techniques to help you cope more effectively. It is a wonderful chance to grow, and therefore, can be a positive thing. Don't waste time berating yourself for momentary failures. Instead, take the time to reflect on the 'denial' you may need to overcome -- so you can move to the next phase. Re-skill yourself with new and better tools.

FEAR OF FAILURE AND FEAR OF SUCCESS

While fear of failure is common in the psychological field, I more often see people who are approaching their goals, suddenly get derailed by a fear of success. Much of this is tied in with their perception of their identity. They have come to know themselves as overspenders, overeaters, gamblers, drinkers, workaholics, or drug users. They sabotage themselves just as they are on the brink of a real change. They do this because they fear the uncertainty of not knowing what their lives will be like when they are successful.

One of my clients, a young man well on his way to successfully losing fifty pounds, put it this way: "Now that I'm getting almost there, I'm afraid that if I am successful in this instance, my parents and teachers are going to ask for repeat performances in different areas! I'm afraid of people making all kinds of new demands on me! When I hear people say 'if you can do this, you can do anything,' I get really scared and I want to go back to the old ways."

Fear of success can be a major roadblock. You need to recognize it and be on the look out to avoid it. It is true there will be some identity transformations as you progress, and it might be helpful to work with a therapist to help you redefine yourself.

I am reminded now of a very successful attorney who had come to me for help. He was earning well over six figures per year, but he was constantly broke or in extreme financial distress. After many interviews, I learned that as soon as he got money in his hands he felt compelled to spend it, to "get rid of it." He felt that "he didn't deserve it, and that one day he was certain to fail and lose everything anyway, so why not just get rid of the money now." Even though he had the drive and intelligence to build a successful career, he still remembered that his brother had always been the "brain" of the family, the sports star, the best-looking and the most rewarded person in the family. From this early life conditioning, he felt that he didn't deserve success -- so even after attaining it through his own hard work and intelligence, he was still trying to "get rid of the success" because he was conditioned to believe that he didn't deserve it.

After much discussion, he came to see himself as a whole person who was deserving of success built on his own merits. No one had the right to put limits on his success.

This is a vitally important point that has the potential of being a major stumbling block in shedding unhealthy habits. I urge you to evaluate your thoughts and perceptions of your "right to have success." If there is a problem, you must think it through clearly, and if necessary, get some counseling to help you through the situation.

FINDING LIFE'S MEANING

Finding a "meaning to life" is very important! This is one of the most vital cornerstones in developing your healthy habits. I want to encourage you to take this concept seriously, particularly if you do not have strong religious ties. If you are involved in a particular religion, you hopefully have found a sense new of tranquility and some important answers through your spiritual beliefs.

On the other hand, if you have not been able to find the kind of solace that you need through religion or otherwise, don't deny it's importance. The meaning of life is one of the single most powerful reasons why people turn to unhealthy habits. I can't tell you how often I hear the words, "Why bother living?" - "I'm going to die anyway. . .I can't think of a reason that would make me want to go on." Each person must face himself/herself and come to grips with the question to find his/her own unique answers.

In the end, your concept of the meaning of life may be very different from that of your birth religion, your family, and your friends. It is important that you know and understand your own meaning, whatever it is.

Some people find direction through volunteer efforts such as charity work where they are actively involved on a one-on-one basis in helping others. For others, having children and a family is what it is all about. Others find the creative life to be their answer, and still others find it in a more spiritual sense. There is no limit to the options -- you have a whole universe of definitions at your disposal. Whichever path you take, whatever answers are right for you, they should and will be your own. Just know that finding some meaning in life is essential in creating 'centerness and peace' in attaining a lasting and stable recovery from practicing unhealthy habits.

FINDING NEW REWARDS

Perhaps the most attractive feature of our unhealthy habits is that they provide a reward at the end of a hard day. We are creatures who were reared on rewards, starting with the cookie that your mother gave you when you behaved well or did something good. We receive diplomas after graduating, paychecks every week and prizes when we are lucky.

I don't know what your particular rewards consist of, but it is important that you give yourself treats to replace the ones you have been used to receiving. As you well know, in healthy lifestyles, rewards do not come in a bottle, a capsule, or any other form of a "short-cut life." Healthy rewards consist of vacations, new clothes, or some desirable item you have had your eye on for a while. I often ask my clients to go immediately to their travel agent and book themselves on a short get-away. That way, when they are feeling the pain of going all week without a drink or without overeating, they will have something pleasurable and tangible to look forward to with anticipation and excitement.

It is easy to tell yourself that you are doing okay, that you don't need vacations, or that you don't have the time or money to go anywhere. But you must! You need that time away -- you need that break -- you need that reward! It is also important to reward yourself frequently. Working hard and making sacrifices so you can take a trip at the end of the year is fine, but since you have been used to indulging in your unhealthy habit on a daily or frequent basis, it is important that you now reward yourself on a more frequent basis in a healthy manner.

Between major rewards, you need to find small ways to treat yourself -- a movie, a play, a concert, a special evening out, a major sporting event, a drive through the country or to the sea, a massage a facial, a manicure -- anything that you value as being special and that will not lead you back to your unhealthy habit.

A fun thing to do, at this time, is to open your own "private bank." Whenever you would have practiced your unhealthy habit, deposit the money you would have spent on it in a jar or special bank account and just watch the money build up. You will be surprised how expensive your unhealthy habit was. When you accumulate enough money, treat yourself to something special that in the past you would not have been able to afford due to the money being spent on your unhealthy behavior.

Another thing that is important is to keep yourself attuned to the rewards which you are getting naturally as a result of giving up your unhealthy lifestyle. They may be small changes at first, but they will become more noticeable as time progresses. Learn to recognize and appreciate these rewards, and realize that your new lifestyle is making them possible.

If you do not find life more rewarding without practicing your unhealthy habits, you will eventually return to them. It doesn't hurt to make a list of all the rewards you will eventually attain. Even if these rewards are not immediately as powerfully reinforcing as your old behavior, realize that together they are adding up and will continue to increase. Know that in time, they will provide more peace and pleasure than your unhealthy habit did, and without the guilt, remorse, and unpleasant side-effects.

Of course, these are techniques that allow you to "Skill Yourself, Instead of Killing Yourself."

TAKING STOCK AGAIN

At this point, you should take the time to complete the following two forms ("How Are You Doing?" and "Developing & Keeping Healthy Structures"). Although you have used these forms before, it is now time to complete them again. It should be interesting to note the changes between the initial and secondary forms. Even if it is only a slight change, it proves that you are breaking out of your "comfort zone" and "building emotional muscle" by making changes in your life. Don't lose your forward momentum, keep making progress!

HOW ARE YOU DOING ?

Rate how satisfied you are presently with the following areas of your life:

-10	-5	0	5	10
Very Dissatisfied	Somewhat Dissatisfied	Neutral	Somewhat Satisfied	Very Satisfied

Career/Employment ....   -10   -5   0   5   10

Friends/Companionship ....   -10   -5   0   5   10

Family ....   -10   -5   0   5   10

Leisure Activities/Hobbies ....   -10   -5   0   5   10

Intimate Relationships ....   -10   -5   0   5   10

Drug or Alcohol Use/Cravings ....   -10   -5   0   5   10

Unhealthy Habit/Cravings ....   -10   -5   0   5   10

Eating Behavior/Cravings ....   -10   -5   0   5   10

Self-Esteem ....   -10   -5   0   5   10

Physical Health ....   -10   -5   0   5   10

Psychological Well-Being ....   -10   -5   0   5   10

Sexual Fulfillment ....   -10   -5   0   5   10

Spiritual Well-Being ....   -10   -5   0   5   10

DEVELOPING AND KEEPING
HEALTHY STRUCTURES

Use the chart below to list those healthy structures that are vital to your continuing recovery. If there are specific people or activities or thoughts you need to avoid, also list those. Refer to this list regularly to check yourself, and to make sure that you are continuing to stay with important positive structures while avoiding negative structures. Remember, developing all the structures you will need may take a long time and many attempts. Keep trying, add new ones as needed, take control and don't give up!

I NEED TO INTEGRATE THESE POSITIVE STRUCTURES.	Date of 1st attempt	Date of 2nd attempt	Date of next attempt	Date structure stabilized

I AM AVOIDING THESE NEGATIVE STRUCTURES.	Date of 1st attempt	Date of 2nd attempt	Date of next attempt	Date structure stabilized

CHAPTER 6 SOME THINGS JUST ARE

PART 3 NOW WE'VE COME FULL CIRCLE

Now that we have followed the roadmap to breaking unhealthy habits and developing healthy behaviors, there are just a couple of things I'd like to add. One point I need to make is that I really do not believe that you ever become "cured" of your most powerful unhealthy habits, rather that you replace them with a more stable, enjoyable, and healthy lifestyle.

I do not want to use the term "recovering" as they do in Alcoholics Anonymous. Instead, I would like you to think of yourself as "continually renewing your life," and making your life as rich and fulfilling as possible. It is comforting to know that in the future there are likely to be new and even better techniques to help you gain more control over certain aspects of your life. Some areas, however, will remain unchangeable and learning to live with them will be the best you can do.

There are two bottom line issues:

(1)   First, you must learn how to tolerate less than optimal, and sometimes even acutely uncomfortable, feelings without using your unhealthy habit.

(2)   Secondly, you must not engage in your unhealthy habit long enough for the norm to become "not engaging in the habit." Another way of saying it is: You must stop the destructive repetition and become comfortable with the new life you create without it. It is an incredibly simple concept, but not at all an easy one to achieve. If you find yourself resistant, you are very likely denying just how hard it is to do those simple things.

If you can learn to do these two simple things, I guarantee you that you will be successful in shedding your unwanted habits -- you have gained the skills that we have discussed so much in our motto: "Don't Kill Yourself, Skill Yourself."

One final word, this book is designed to be read and referred to over and over again. Use it, photo copy all the charts, and highlight with a marker, the most relevant points for yourself. Make it one of your best friends, and it will help you through many rough spots and lead you to the pathway of success!

TAKE CONTROL NOW!

EPILOGUE

"You're On Your Way"

You have now received the tools that have the capacity to give you the power to embrace and understand feelings and reality, and to accept the sharp corners and rough edges of life without losing control. You should no longer have to live a secret life, practicing the unhealthy habits that have put a wall around you and forced you to live alone.

Through this encounter with Dr. Kern, you have learned that it was not your fault that you fell prey to a secret "short-cut life." You now can understand that you were seduced and led into unhealthy habits by a long series of circumstances beyond your control. You need no longer be the victim! You have been exposed to the tools that will help you to build 'emotional muscle' which will allow you to attain that true, healthy control that you have always wanted. Believe in yourself, discard the secret life, shed the darkness -- Let the light into your life! Now, you have the knowledge to develop and nourish the inner strength to love, and understand yourself and to share that self with others in an honest, satisfying and productive manner.

Let this be the dawning of a resilient, well-equipped, emotionally stable Human Being who is in control -- capable of dealing with himself/herself and the world. This is not the illusion of control, it is genuine control!

Yes, there is an answer. The answer was and will always be YOU! You have the knowledge to create a world for yourself that is meaningful and satisfying, and Dr. Kern has put the key in your hand that unlocks your unlimited skills that have been suppressed. Use this book always! Never slip backward! Remember, whenever you begin to feel shackled by life, you have the keys on the pages of this book to unlock those shackles. Let this book be your guide to mental security and health. Rely upon your Unique Factor, and continue to be a loving individual who has rights and gives understanding, and you will have mastered your own life well.

"Skill Yourself, Don"t Kill Yourself!"

TAKE CONTROL, NOW!